TABLE OF CONTENTS

DEDICATION

To my mother, Lois Wilson Young,
and my "other mom," Phyllis Taylor Cleaver,
two women whose managements of their households
reflect godly priorities and whose entrepreneurial efforts
have benefited all their children in spirit and character

WORK AT HOME OPTIONS

JOANNE CLEAVER

LIFEJOURNEY
BOOKS
A Division of Cook Communications

Chariot Books™ is an imprint of David C. Cook Publishing Co.
David C. Cook Publishing Co., Elgin, Illinois 60120
David C. Cook Publishing Co., Weston, Ontario
Nova Distribution Ltd., Eastbourne, England

WORK AT HOME OPTIONS
© 1994 by Joanne Cleaver

Cover design by Eric Walljasper
Cover illustration by Johnston Clark
First printing, 1994
Printed in U.S.A.
98 97 96 95 94   5 4 3 2 1
 CIP applied for/LC number

❖

Introduction

WELCOME TO MY OFFICE . . . playroom . . . study
This is not one of those slick, white-laminate designer offices that home magazines love to feature. The personal computers sit on garage sale desks. The secondhand lateral file is criss-crossed with markers, thanks to an acting-out two year old. Legal pads are piled on a table along with Dr. Seuss books; the pencil can is decorated with a kindergartener's crayon picture.

Just to reach the working part, you have to maneuver through a subdivision of Fisher-Price people, tiptoe over chalk spilt on the floor, and skirt around drifted piles of construction paper.

Is this any way to run a career?

You bet.

Over and over again, people have told me that working from home is the best of both worlds. Yes, I reply, and it's also the stress of both worlds. It's lonely and crowded at the same time. There's always too much work to do in any direction I turn. To get to my third-floor office I have to walk past unmade beds, un-put-away clothes, and a bathroom that's always smeared with gobs of toothpaste. Professional and maternal roles are often on a collision course.

And I'm thoroughly convinced that this is God's provision for our family.

If the kitchen is the heart of the home, then the home workplace is its brain. It's where my preschooler plays while I make business calls. It's where our fourth and seventh graders do much of their homework while I catch up on writing and filing. It's where my husband, Mark, and I, swiveled away from our respective computers and, concentrating on each other, have some of our most intimate late-evening discussions of our hopes and goals.

Families, especially those with God as the head, do not have to be worn down by the apparently diametrically opposed priorities of work and family. When you make a decision, as we have, that rearing children in the fear of the Lord is a primary call that is subjugated only to marriage and one's personal spiritual walk, God responds with grace and generosity. He has for my family, and He will for yours.

I've met dozens of families attracted to the home-work lifestyle. Working from home offers the chance to have a steady, substantial income while participating in the joys and responsibilities of being at home during the day. However, it can be a complicated endeavor that delivers not peace but pressure; where the home represents hassles, not a haven.

How do you know if you're cut out for home work? Ultimately, there's no way to find out without trying it. But you can benefit from the experience of those who are already walking down this path.

A primary purpose of this book is to give you a well-rounded idea of what it's really like to work from home, so that you can evaluate your own family's goals and situation and arrive at the work life-style solution that is right for you. I hope that you'll find inspiration and encouragement from the hearts of other families who've wrestled with the frustrating realities of trying to find income-producing work that does not undermine everyday family life.

My challenge to you is to use this book to develop a business plan that equips you to achieve success with your spiritual, personal, and financial goals.

·1·

Be Realistic—Expect an Everyday Miracle

SOMETIMES I THINK it's a miracle that my friend Theresa makes it through the day. She thinks so too. If the phrase "every mother is a working mother" was coined for anyone, that person is Theresa.

She has six children ranging from a toddler to an eleven year old (and including preschool twins). She is heavily involved in counseling students who come through her family's connections with a local campus ministry and she is a member of her church's oversight council. Doesn't this woman have enough jobs? But on top of all of this, she spends about twenty hours a week managing several apartment buildings, including the one her family occupies.

"I did not start this thing for self-fulfillment," Theresa says with dry understatement. "Sure, working is stressful. But not being able to pay the bills was even more stressful."

In 1987, Theresa and her husband, Robb, were facing some difficult financial realities. The bottom line was that no amount of coupon clipping, bulk buying, or helpful hand-me-downs would make the frayed ends of their budget meet.

At the same time, Theresa's father was searching for a way to invest in income-producing real estate. Though her engineering degree overqualified her to work as a property manager, Theresa and her father felt that her low-key temperament and basic understanding of the way mechanical things work made her a good candidate for the job. The fact that she would be helping build her family's equity and establish retirement security for her parents clinched the deal. Theresa's father purchased apartment buildings totaling twenty-eight units. One of them, a three-flat, is partially owned and occupied by Theresa's family.

In a typical workweek, a woman who lives with the family in exchange for light housekeeping and child care looks after Theresa's preschoolers for about twelve hours. Theresa uses that time to concentrate on the complex tax work and bookkeeping inherent in property management, run errands to the bank and hardware store, show apartments, meet with contractors, and occasionally take a deadbeat tenant to court.

After some initial renovation, the buildings are now producing an annual cash flow of $150,000. Of that, Theresa receives eight percent, or about $13,000—the standard in the industry. Though she has to deduct about $2,000 annually for office supplies, phone service , and child-care expenses, the family "just couldn't make it" without that $11,000. Theresa sees the fortuitously timed arrangement with her father as God's provision and care for both her family and her parents.

"For a few years, I was one-third of our budget," she says. "If I didn't have this job, I don't know what we'd do."

Modern-Day Myths

You can have it all. You can't have it all. Having it all is too much. Not trying to have it all is wimping out. Okay, don't try to have it all—but don't blame me if you aren't fulfilled.

In a nutshell, that's a brief summary of the women's work-related headlines that have appeared in the press in the last fifteen years. Every nuance of the working mother trend has been publicly analyzed by reporters, pop psychologists and sociologists, academics, and consultants (not to mention grandmas). Virtually every American employer has had to deal with the issue, some successfully, most not.

For all the discussion and raw emotion swirling around the topic of working mothers, there's one thing that's rarely examined: just what is the "it all" that moms can or can't try to have?

The "having it all" role model that is typically presented to the public is a high-profile high achiever with two picture-perfect kids, a designer wardrobe (size six), a sparkling house, and an admiring, supportive husband. What the magazine articles don't tell you is that this woman is her own cottage industry. She employs a full-time nanny and a housekeeper and has a whole support staff at work. Her hairdresser, manicurist, and personal shopper meet her in her office over lunch so she doesn't have to waste any time running errands. She doesn't have to pull globs of hair out of the bathroom sink, is never late to work because her toddler has cleverly hidden his gym shoes (again), and is never too tired to have an intimate evening with her husband, complete with scented candles and silk sheets.

This is not real life for ninety-nine percent of all moms, whether they work for pay or not. That's why this neo-fairy tale fell out of favor by the late 1980s. Juggling career and home responsibilities is extremely stressful, and inevitably some of those balls get dropped. Parents searching for better ways to invest in their children and still maintain financial security are propelling the major trend of the 1990s—alternative career tracks.

Redefining "it all," first in God's terms and then in the terms that fit the particular needs of your family, is a must for families searching for a permanent, frequently home-based, work situation for the mother. In the following chapters, we'll see how a wide variety of situations work out for parents with very different educational and experiential backgrounds and long-term expectations.

For many, working at home is the ideal solution, either as an entrepreneur or as a long-distance employee. Some prefer to develop a home-based position that involves some out-of-the home meetings, calls, and local travel. The best situation for others is a flexible variation of part-time hours or responsibilities within the parameters of a traditional office.

The thread that runs through all the situations described in this book is that every parent prayerfully pursued the options and opportunities that they saw God opening to them. We'll find out how they decided whether or not home-based work was right for their families. Then we'll learn about the steps they took to create the situation that they desired. How did they work out the child-care question? What successes and disappointments have they encountered in a home-based career or a flexible arrangement away from home? Most importantly, in what ways has God responded to their faith in His promise of provision for their families?

The Big Picture (from an Earthly Point of View)

In my work as a reporter and writer, I introduce myself over the phone to dozens of people each week. Upon hearing my last name, three out of four feel compelled to ask, "How's the Beave?"

To most of these people, the Cleaver family of the 1950s sitcom "Leave It to Beaver" is a fondly remembered anachronism. Everybody knows (they think) that those days of omniscient Dad and happy homemaker Mom are about as relevant to life in the 1990s as the Edsel, another 1950s newsmaker. The Cleavers are constantly cited by my colleagues in the media as a prime example of exactly what life in the 1990s isn't. Statistics are continually paraded before us to "prove" that only reactionaries think that the nuclear family is still the norm.

We're told that we just can't manage on one income the way Ward and June did. And women shouldn't define themselves by their mundane accomplishments at home, but must attain self-fulfillment through career advancement. Kids should be independent anyway, and don't necessarily need or want Mom and Dad hanging around dispensing gems of homely wisdom with the homemade cookies. Quality time is more important than quantity time.

A parallel contemporary attitude deifies childhood as inherently pure and innocent—and declares it the parents' responsibility to make sure that each child is served a full plate of potential-enhancing opportunities. These are popularly defined as the "right" education (whether it's public, private, or home school), myriad enrichment classes, camps, and field trips. Parents who buy into this attitude are addicted to a constant stream of advice from experts on everything from eco-correct diapers to financing college. This preoccupation with creating the perfect childhood makes parents virtual slaves to their children.

At-home mothers are on a treadmill of volunteer responsibilities, car pools, and play-with-a-purpose. Families with two full-time earners are even further behind, as they have to pay a caretaker to do for minimum wage what they themselves do only for love (when they have time). And pity the frazzled single parents with the worst of both worlds: usually unable to keep up with the pint-sized Joneses, and painfully aware of it.

I'm not going to tackle all the faulty assertions of media-induced popular wisdom here. However, it's important to understand what these self-appointed experts are trying to justify.

Things Seem So Much More Expensive Because They Are

The basic economics of the American household have changed dramatically in just one generation. Until the 1970s, a single bread-winner could not only support a family and a mortgage, he could pull his family's life-style up with him as he climbed the corporate ladder. Incessant inflation, steadily rising taxes at every governmental level, and increased standard-of-living norms have all but eroded those expectations.

Social Security taxes have increased 150 percent in the last twenty years—and that figure is adjusted for inflation. According to the Tax Foundation, state and local taxes, including property taxes, went up 30 percent from 1980 to 1991, after inflation. In the same period, the average federal income tax decreased 9 percent and middle-class income increased only 10 percent—gains that hardly balanced out the higher taxes. According to an analysis of Census Bureau statistics by the Joint Economic Committee staff, real hourly pay, adjusted for inflation, actually declined between 1979 and 1989 for 60 percent of husbands in two-parent families. Families maintained their standard of living only because wives returned to work, (initially) making some gains in income.

Economist Sylvia Ann Hewlett reports that mortgage payments now eat up 29 percent of median family income, up from 17 percent in 1970. Tuition for the average four-year college education is 40 percent of the average family's income, up from 29 percent in 1970. The proportion of families purchasing a home on a single income fell from 47 percent in 1976 to 21 percent in 1989, according to a survey conducted by Chicago Title and Trust.

Social (and Economic) Insecurity

Fewer and fewer families can make it on one income. That's not a political statement or a call to socialist or welfare-state arms. It's economic reality.

You need only to consult your local newspaper or a national news magazine to find out where all that tax money is going. Starting with the depression-induced New Deal, all levels of government have dramatically expanded both their roles and their taxing authorities. Simply put, with all other things being equal, the government is consuming more of your paycheck than it did of your dad's.

Excepting those in the very top income brackets, few families are able to manage on a single paycheck. Most that do, make significant trade-offs to do so, like two of my close friends from college. Brad and Debbie, parents of six children, found themselves unable to keep pace with the cost of living in metropolitan Chicago. They moved to a very small town and bought a three-bedroom fixer-upper. Their mortgage is less than their rent was in the city. Brad commutes two hours each day to his job as a computer programmer on the suburban fringe. Debbie home-schools the children, cans and freezes bushels of vegetables each summer from her garden, and sews most of their clothes. They're perfectly happy with their life choices, but they recognize that the circumstances that are right for them wouldn't necessarily work for other equally committed Christian families.

In the 1980s, additional factors complicated the economic scene and its impact on families. United States corporations wrestled with complex issues of global competition; numerous management-theory fads swept through corporate boardrooms; and corporations were constantly restructuring (to use the euphemism of the decade, "downsizing"). The net effect of all this change was to undermine the faith that American workers had in their corporate leaders and in the work ethic itself. No longer is it true that if you work hard and keep your nose clean, you'll always have a job. Millions of highly productive, loyal employees discovered with a shock that their efforts did not necessarily count in the midst of a restructuring.

Rhetoric and Reality

Added to these economic realities was a generous helping of feminist rhetoric. A basic plank in the early feminist platform was that women deserved equal access and opportunity in school and in the work force—a concept that is only common sense. But as women entered previously male-dominated schools, professions, and positions, the rhetoric shifted. Equality was taken for granted, and the revised philosophy claims that women need careers to be fulfilled and to completely partake of life. In fact, in some circles women who choose to scale back or abandon career aspirations for the sake of their families are held in contempt as male-dominated pawns or traitors to the cause.

At the same time, many women have found real enjoyment and satisfaction at a "regular job." It's just as silly to pretend that most women lose complete interest and enjoyment in their job skills once they have a family as it is to force them all into the same nine-to-five mold. If you're experienced, confident, and just plain talented at a particular career, and it helps support your family as well, it seems a waste to completely chuck it once the babies start arriving. (Personally, I find it a relief to have projects to be completed in the near future—something between the endless daily chores and the very long-term objective of rearing well-adjusted, productive citizens. Once I finish a story, I never have to write it again—something that can't be said for making dinner or picking up the family room.)

Given these sweeping changes in attitude and reality, it's not hard to see why journalists, consultants, academicians, and researchers feel that they are doing the public a favor by continuing to present working mothers not as a norm, but as *the* norm. The fact that many journalists are working mothers and know only people with life-styles and viewpoints similar to their own only reinforces their myopia.

This skewed viewpoint has resulted in an equally skewed "generally accepted wisdom." For example, one ubiquitous statistic used as a rationale for everything from the need for more government-financed day-care centers to marketing strategies for new brands of pantyhose is this: about 67 percent of all mothers with children under age eighteen work.

That's absolutely true. But that figure, derived from ongoing United States Department of Labor surveys, includes Tupperware ladies, lawyers, substitute teachers, women who only work at the family store during the Christmas rush, people who make craft items and sell them at regional fairs, and on and on. While I have chosen a home-based career that provides enough flexibility that my preschooler spends only about ten hours a month in child care, I'm lumped in that "67 percent of working moms" category with a hard-driving product manager whose typical workday starts with a power breakfast at 7:00 A.M. and ends at 6:00 P.M. with a networking meeting.

That's just one example of how quick, simple statistics obscure complex life choices. Many mothers are working. But they are not all working in the same fashion or with the same set of priorities. Yet, the self-perpetrating "67 percent of all mothers work" myth does not differentiate among them.

A more accurate reflection of mothers' work habits is revealed by a 1992 poll by FEMALE (Formerly Employed Mothers at the Leading Edge), a national association of at-home moms. Though they identify themselves primarily by their family priorities, 39 percent of FEMALE members work an average of fourteen hours per week, and 78 percent intend to eventually return to full-time employment. Another national group, Mothers at Home, recently surveyed the fifteen thousand women who subscribe to its newsletter and found that 48 percent earned some income, many from home-based businesses.

Homing in on the Solution

In the mid-1980s, technology caught up with working mothers, and a new trend was born. Frustrated with the daily headaches of sending children to child care, dealing with corporate bureaucracies for fifty hours a week, and not even having enough time to iron a blouse, women with several years' work experience began to venture out on their own. This in itself is nothing new—about the same percentage of male middle managers walk away from corporate life in mid-career (roughly ages thirty-five to forty-five, and usually to start their own companies). However, unlike most of the men, many women are motivated by a deep desire to regain control over their work and bring it back into balance with their family life.

Home-based work is rapidly gaining acceptance as the premiere business trend of the decade. Ironically, the same corporate layoffs that caused so much turmoil and grief have also fueled a much greater acceptance of home-based work. Many managers and highly trained staff people who suddenly found themselves without jobs have either become self-employed or launched businesses at home. Their numbers and qualifications automatically boosted the home worker image. Even if displaced executives subsequently rejoined the downtown corporate world or if their businesses eventually outgrew their houses, their experience ingrained in many of them a respect for home-based workers and a willingness to take them seriously. The upheaval caused by corporate restructuring also forced big companies to reexamine their set-in-concrete personnel policies.

And many women, frustrated by the narrow career paths offered by most corporations, challenged the status quo. Institutional solutions, such as corporate or government-run child-care centers and "sick child care," don't ease the emotional conflict that most mothers (and some fathers) feel about leaving their children for full-time work. A recent survey by Yankelovich Clancey Shulman indicated that for the first time in twenty years, mothers' desire to persist in the full-time work force has started to erode. When asked if they'd stay home with their children if they could afford it, 56 percent of the mothers surveyed said yes. In the late 1980s, when female careerism was peaking, only 33 percent responded that way. Increasingly, parents see flexibility—both in when and where they accomplish their work—as the answer. The demand for flexible work options is only bound to increase as pressures mount on the "sandwich generation"—families carrying the twin burdens of caring for children at home and for aging parents.

No revolution has happened yet. According to the *Numbers News*, only 2-6 percent of all full-time workers in major metropolitan areas are home-based. Still, executives are warming up to the ideas of career-track part-time work, job sharing, compressed work weeks, and regular relationships with independent contractors. A 1992 study by Hay/Huggins, a benefits consulting firm, found that 36 percent of large American companies officially offer flexible hours policies; as well, 14 percent offer employees a telecommuting option.

There is mounting evidence that more people than ever are experimenting with at-home and flexible work arrangements. According to the Bureau of Labor Statistics, the number of professionals voluntarily working part-time has increased 29 percent from 1983 to 1991, from 1.7 million to 2.2 million. The research firm Link Resources, Inc., reports that 31 percent of the total work force is home-based (that includes part-timers and second jobs for full-time workers).

"Is that a baby I hear in the background? How old is she? Oh, we have one that age, too!"

As a business reporter, I've noticed a shift in attitude on the part of the people I interview as I'm researching a story. When I first started free-lancing in 1981, I took great pains to hide the fact that I worked from my home office. Occasionally, someone on the other end of the phone line would comment that he could hear my baby in the background. (Despite my best efforts to schedule calls during nap times, people didn't always call back when all was calm.)

Cringing, I'd admit that, yes, I was working from my home office that day. A few people pressed for details: Did I do this regularly? How had I gotten started? How did I work out child care? Frequently, my interviewee would sigh and say, "My wife wants to do what you do. Can she call you?"

These days people are just as likely to return my call from a car, plane, or their home as they are from the office. Frequently, executives with enough corporate clout to be an official press spokesperson operate from their homes on certain days. And I'm no longer apologetic about working from home. If I need to ask someone to hold on while I turn down the background blare of *The Little Mermaid* soundtrack, I joke about it—if the caller isn't singing along with the tape.

It's not that professionalism has taken a back seat. Instead, I'm sufficiently confident in my reputation as a sharp, fair reporter that I don't think the location of my workplace has anything to do with the quality of my work. Any source that thinks he'll be tossed some puffballs because I'm sitting in a home office is quickly disabused of that notion. And I have a ready comeback for the few intransigent souls whose voices have an edge of skepticism when they deduce that I'm working from home: I tell them I telecommute, which is true, because I transmit my stories by modem. Telecommuting is so "cutting edge" that it immediately eliminates any trace of anti-homism!

We're Not Talking Macrame and Tie-Dye

In the early 1980s, when the advent of personal computers launched a wave of predictions about the "electronic cottage," work-from-home carried with it strong connotations of grandmas crocheting Barbie doll clothes to sell at the county fair. Today, according to BIS Strategic Decisions, a market research firm, crafts manufacture makes up only 4.4 percent of home enterprise. The overwhelming number of home-based enterprises—70 percent—are services: accounting, desktop publishing, educating, and consulting.

About half these services are aimed at consumers, with the other half targeting businesses as their customers.

Retail sales accounts for 11.8 percent. This category includes mail order as well as direct selling, such as Avon, Tupperware, and Discovery Toys. BIS predicts that the biggest home-work growth areas are business and financial consulting, catering, and niche services.

The United States Department of Labor estimates that demand for self-employed management analysts will increase 47 percent between now and the year 2005; the demand for home-based secretarial and other clerical support workers will grow an estimated 25 percent.

A Faith Odyssey

In the midst of all this workplace upheaval are the eternal truths of the Bible. Twentieth-century trends, be they family-friendly or destructive, do not affect God's eternal purpose for our families. As people who take to heart God's desire to be our Father and provider, it's idolatry for us to look to any man-made institution to care for us.

The era of the Daddy Warbucks-type of corporation mindset is over. Dying with it are expectations of lifelong employment, generous benefit and pension packages, and the false security of the corporate "family."

Few rational people, Christian or not, truly believe that it's healthy to depend on the government as the de facto head of the household. And independence is healthy only so long as it does not degenerate into a self-worship that undermines the softness of spirit that keeps us humbly following in Jesus' footsteps.

As enjoyable as it is to welcome home-work as a trend that appears to reinforce biblical family values, home-work in itself is no substitute for faith in God. It's tempting to breathe a sigh of relief that, finally, here is the solution to the conflicts of financial and family needs. But if you put your trust in the vehicle of God's blessing, instead of in Him, it is as much a sin as believing blindly in a corporation, a government, or yourself.

With that caveat in mind, it's very possible that some sort of flexible employment arrangement will be the direct answer to your heartfelt prayers. In fact, your biggest challenge may be settling on the best of the several options open to you. The particulars of God's provision for your family will unfold as you pursue Him first and rely on Him to work out the details. When your circumstances shift, expect that God will fine-tune your work to accommodate them. He is the only constant in this world of incessant change.

In the Beginning

From personal experience, I can assure you that home-based work is no panacea. There are still issues of control, tension, and frustration with things not going the way you want them to. The nadir of my work-from-home experience came early on. After several days of phone tag, I'd finally connected with a New York advertising agency executive whose comments were crucial to a story I was working on. Just as he and I started to dig into the interview, my oldest daughter, then two-and-a-half and in potty training, woke from her nap. For some reason, she chose to take off her underwear. Then she sidled into my office, leaned against my leg and—yes, she did—pooped down my leg and onto the peach-colored carpet. The interview continued without missing a beat, but the carpet never recovered. Fortunately, most of my attempts to mesh family life and at-home-work have been more successful.

I remember the tension that characterized my first several years of free-lance work. When I unexpectedly became pregnant in December 1980, I was in the middle of my journalism master's program. Mark and I had been married for only six months. I confidently assured my panic-stricken husband that I'd just free-lance instead of entering the work force full-time.

It was all bluff, though I didn't have the guts to tell him that until a couple of years ago. My long-term career strategy had been to become invaluable to a trade or business magazine and then to carry that relationship forward into a telecommuting or free-lance position when we began a family. Starting from scratch, fresh from grad school, trying to make a good first impression wearing a yellow linen maternity jumper and blazer over a big round tummy, did not seem like an auspicious start. (At least I didn't start retaining water around my ankles until my interviews with editors were over.)

The years proved not only that God's provision is faithful and consistent, but also that He has a sense of humor. While in college, I'd interned for three consecutive summers with the trade magazine of the country's largest savings and loan trade association. That experience was enough to get me in the door at Crain's Chicago Business, one of the country's premier weekly business newspapers, when it was only three years old. While assignments and relationships at Crain's gained momentum (and continue strong to this day), work from the savings and loan magazine tapered off to nothing. I can only imagine where my career would be if I had stubbornly pursued the association magazine as a primary source of income. The national scandals that rocked the S & L business in the late 1980s reverberated through the association and all its publications, with a net loss of many jobs.

As I settled in each morning at my desk sandwiched between the playpen and a file cabinet in a corner of our apartment dining room, I had to make a conscious decision to turn that day's work over to Jesus. There was too much at stake to do anything else. Every time I got a call from an editor for an assignment, I felt like throwing a party. I'd feverishly work and rework each assignment, acutely aware that in the free-lance arena, you're only as good as your last story. My operating philosophy was, and still is, to do what's necessary (within reasonable parameters) to make the editor look good to his boss. Many times we had take-out pizza for dinner because I was fact-checking right up to deadline.

As I saw and felt the Lord's protection week after week, story after story, I gradually relaxed. Confidence in His good intentions for our family and in my own experience began to replace my nagging fears of somehow blowing it. When I did have a short and scary run of published errors one spring, God in His sovereignty protected my credibility with my editor. I didn't hide or minimize my very public mistakes. I made the appropriate apologies and amends and carried on as graciously as I could.

The Prayer Day-timer

My career ambition has been tempered by my greater desire to be a godly wife and mother. Aside from planned maternity leaves and vacations, I have had exactly one week without writing assignments. It all has come as a direct result of my continuous prayer to remain in submission to God's greater will and purpose for my life. I want to take full advantage of the opportunities He brings to me. I also strive to relinquish to Him control over the flow of work and other responsibilities and situations He brings into my life.

The times that I sent out dozens of story proposals to regional and national magazines and got only rejection letters coincided with periods when I needed to divert more energy to working with my husband on leading a small group, or spend time with family members in crisis, or concentrate on helping a daughter through a complicated phase of development. (Toilet training and deadlines don't mix!)

Likewise, the Lord has made it abundantly clear which projects He has wanted me to pursue. Many writers spend year after frustrating year trying to get their proposals or manuscripts even read by book editors. In winter 1988, within five weeks of sending out proposals for a national children's museum guidebook, I had a contract.

When I thought there was a market for a family day- and weekend-trip guidebook for the Chicago area, a single proposal to one local publisher resulted in a contract. (I've since produced, expanded, and updated second editions of each book.)

Not incidentally, the research period for *Somewhere Over the Dan Ryan, Day and Weekend Outings for Chicago Area Families* coincided with construction that rendered our backyard almost useless for the entire summer of 1989. Even though I was carting around an eight year old, five year old, and baby to all the 125 sites reviewed in the book, it sure beat staying at home!

My favorite example of God's sovereign timing involves a wretchedly rundown house and a Swedish packaging manufacturer. In September 1985, we moved into the house we'd been praying over for months. The key word to describe this house was "potential." It had holes in the ceilings, huge jagged cracks in the walls, a leaky roof, hideously paneled bathrooms and kitchen, and walls painted in neon shades. Its primary virtues were that it was big and cheap.

Brimming with naive enthusiasm, we plunged into rehabbing our house with the princely (we thought) sum of ten thousand dollars. It was gone in a week. The roof, floors, plaster work, carpet and painting consumed it all, and we had not even touched any of the major projects. My husband and I were stunned, fighting a desperate feeling in our guts that this house was going to eat us alive.

One phone call—probably my single strangest divine appointment—changed it all and brought our vision of God's abundance back in line. Just before we'd moved, I'd gotten a phone call out of the blue from the director of public relations for a Swedish company that had just set up an American subsidiary. She was looking for an American business journalist to ghostwrite the company's quarterly marketing newsletter, which went out to customers and suppliers describing the many uses and advantages of the company's packaging products. I'd forwarded to her the usual set of writing samples and my résumé. Then, for the only time in my life, I'd actually forgotten all about the prospect.

But the director called one week after we moved. I was hired; the paperwork for the first issue was in the mail; when could I fly to the plant and research facility for a tour and corporate briefing; and how much money did I want for this? Stunned, I gave her a figure triple what I'd have charged if I'd really thought about it, figuring I'd settle for a lesser amount after negotiating. As I subsequently discovered, negotiating was not her style. She was addicted to making snap decisions. The figure I blurted out was what I got.

For the next three years, I churned out copy for the newsletter. The corporate culture was sufficiently bizarre that I felt I more than earned my fee. We remodeled two bathrooms and the attic and started in on the kitchen, much of it directly supported by those earnings.

In 1988, my patience with the arrangement was wearing very thin. In fact, I dreaded the work. And, just as abruptly as the project had entered my life, it disappeared. The public relations director was transferred to London, and her replacement axed the newsletter. It dropped from my consciousness, and the money was made up by book royalties. Fortunately, most of the work on the house was completed by then.

How could I possibly have known to pray for such a situation? I didn't, specifically. But you can believe that my heart was "groaning without words" (Rom. 8:26) when our dream of rehabbing a run-down turn-of-the-century house degenerated into a messy, expensive reality.

Our family's needs are no more known to God than those of your family. He meets our needs before we even fully know what they are, and surely in ways much richer than we can imagine.

My friend Theresa and I, and the other parents whom you'll meet in the following pages, have found that when things look bleak, God comes through. He doesn't want us to buy into the false choice of family or work. Through prayer, research, honest self-evaluation, and focused hard work, you can discern and pursue the work style that best fits His purposes for your family.

❖ 2 ❖

Why Are You Doing This?

AFTER FOURTEEN YEARS of marriage, Posy was caught by surprise. The much-prayed-for hope of her heart was going to be fulfilled. She and her husband were finally going to have a child.

She knew right away that her whole life was going to be reordered. Though she taught full time, she'd also developed a line of handmade Christmas ornaments that were sold in prestigious New York City department stores. She'd have to make some major decisions about what would go and what would stay when the baby came.

When Kyser (now eleven) arrived, Posy had already decided to stay home with him. She resigned her teaching job and transferred her craft business to some fellow teachers who'd already been helping with it. But she found that she couldn't turn off her creative instincts quite that easily.

By defining microniches in the crafts market, she has gradually developed two separate lines of do-it-yourself kits—Christian-themed playthings and children's accessories—and counted-cross-stitch kits that depict American architectural landmarks and historical sites. Until recently Posy also edited an inspirational and how-to newsletter for home-based workers that was started by another entrepreneurial mom.

Of course, this did not all happen at once. When Kyser was eighteen months old, Posy tackled the problem of coming up with a nativity set that he could play with.

"We only had a porcelain one. I commissioned a wooden one (nativity figures cut from felt and appliquéed, as it were, onto wooden blocks) and sold the directions for making it," says Posy. "Kyser started needing other things in his spiritual life, and I just started to make them. One of my philosophies is that if you unselfishly give, you will be blessed. My first goal was to serve my own child. Then other people said they'd like [a nativity pattern] and it turned into something I made money on."

The line has been expanded to include items such as a cross-stitched Sunday school tote bag and a keepsake Advent stocking.

At about the same time that the nativity set developed, Posy and her sister happened to visit Monticello, Thomas Jefferson's historic Virginia home. Posy brought along a handmade wreath to show the buyer at the museum's gift shop. She wanted to find out if there might be a market for such products. He wasn't interested, but Posy persisted, asking him about other needs.

"One of the things I've learned is that if nothing is clicking in a sales meeting, just be quiet and say, 'Well, what are people asking for that you are having problems finding?' " she says.

When she asked that question at the gift shop, the buyer immediately poured out a tale of woe about counted cross-stitch charts. He'd only been able to find one with a historical theme, and the woman who made up the kits wouldn't even stitch a model to hang in the shop so that customers could see how the finished product would look. Customers regularly asked about kits with Monticello on them.

"My husband said, 'I think it's time for you to do something with this!' " Posy laughs. She wasn't skilled in developing cross-stitch charts, but her sister was. On the other hand, because of her experience selling to New York department stores, Posy was confident she could develop a marketing strategy and sell the kits—the last thing her sister wanted to do.

A partnership formed on the spot. The line now includes more than sixty-five designs and is carried by museum shops all along the Eastern seaboard.

"People sometimes say, 'Oh, you just got a break.' Well, yeah, I did get a break, but I also made a lot of phone calls," Posy says. "I believe that God is in charge of my life. He has a plan for me, but I don't think He wants me to sit on my hands and wait for it to fall out of a tree. No matter what you're doing, what business you're in, there are things you can do while you wait. That's when you make your own luck."

Though marketing—both perceiving the unfilled niche and convincing shop buyers that her company is the one to fill it—comes easily to Posy, she says that she depends daily on God to direct her efforts.

"I like doing workshops for churches where they can't pay me, because I'm always amazed at the blessing that comes from it," she relates. "Last December I did a seminar for a church women's group. Afterwards I had some things to sell. No one bought, and no one subscribed to the newsletter, so I decided to go over to Sturbridge Village [an internationally known living history village in central Massachusetts]. It was only open for another hour.

"I went over to check out their gift shop, and it happened to be the day of an annual meeting of top buyers for museum shops in New England. I hadn't known anything about it. I got four new accounts for my cross-stitch kits. I felt that God really placed me there."

According to Posy, contact with the subscribers to the newsletter has sharpened her own motivations for working from home.

"I think it's really easy to tell when people are just wishing," she says. "I hear from people who want to work from home for someone else and make a lot of money. They don't get it. Nobody's going to get rich doing this. The only I reason that I came home is to rear Kyser."

Posy recommends that anyone considering launching a home-based business immediately start researching the markets she is interested in. After finding people in the field with beneficial knowledge, take them out to lunch, specifically asking their advice on distribution, sources, marketing, and other issues. Posy made the acquaintance of the owner of a local Christmas-themed gift shop when she was just beginning to experiment with hand-crafted ornaments. Impressed with Posy's initiative, the shop owner let her place a few designs at a time in the store, effectively using it as a test market. Once Posy saw what would sell, what wouldn't, and at what prices, she was equipped to broaden her marketing efforts.

"You need to recognize the people in your path who will help you," she says. "Then you need to act on your opportunities.

"Having two of my three business be Christian-related is just the biggest joy I have," she says. "I feel that I'm serving people with values similar to mine. And with the museum shops, I'm working with places that further our country's history, which is very meaningful."

What's the Purpose behind the Activity?

What motivates Posy to so diligently pursue her home-based businesses? Originally, she needed to replace her teaching income. She's also a fountain of creativity, spilling over with ideas for new products, new markets, and new ways to communicate her faith and knowledge about working from home. It's just natural for her to translate her creative ideas into marketable products. Most importantly, she was determined to stay home with Kyser and order her work life around her family's needs.

Like Posy, most of us work for a variety of reasons. Before delving into the particulars of home-based work options, it's important that you take a big step back and examine your motivations. Knowing why you want to work from home clears the path for subsequent decisions: what kind of home-work alternative best fits your goals; what kind of temperament, skills, and abilities you have that will make you successful; and how you define success. After all, if you're unclear about where you're going, you may not get where you want to be—or you may get there and not know it!

A common refrain in the secular press is that working is essential to developing self-esteem. They've almost got it straight! Work is ordained by God, whether it's done for money, love, or both. Effort put forth as a "living sacrifice" to the Lord is a pleasant fragrance to Him (Rom. 12:1). Especially if you thrive in a competitive corporate environment, or if you are highly skilled or talented and thoroughly enjoy what you do, work is enjoyable and an important part of who you are.

What's the Source of Your Self-Esteem?

However, work is not the primary source of self-esteem for one living a Christ-centered life. Developing character, growing in the fruits of the Spirit, and nurturing the disciplines of daily Christian walk are the roots of genuine self-worth and maturity. A healthy attitude toward work results from healthy self-esteem, not the other way around.

People who define themselves largely by their jobs are relying on an exterior frame of reference to tell them what they are worth. When that frame of reference changes or is eliminated, through major job shifts or losing a job, these folks are shaken to their core. No wonder—they've lost more than just their income. Their self-concept is built on an unstable foundation and when it cracks, the damage is felt throughout their entire life.

Likewise, these folks can easily fall into pride and self-importance when things are going well at work. A positive desire to respect authority can gradually slip into a slavish adherence to company-established goals and a desire to gain the bosses' approval above all else.

If you have a tendency to define your self-worth through your work, rather than drawing on Jesus as your source of life, simply changing the place where you work will not alleviate the stresses you feel. Let's say, for instance, that you are exhausted from trying to be a super achiever in a company-wide sales competition, and that a high point of your year has been attending the company-sponsored incentive trip for the winners. You've been a big shot in the sales department, and you've told yourself that all the extra hours have actually benefited your marriage because it's resulted in extra income and the perk of a free vacation.

But you also feel that your children's childhood is slipping away and you increasingly are frustrated by the pressure forced on you by corporate management to constantly outdo last year's performance. Simply quitting and becoming an independent sales rep, operating from a home-based office may relieve some of the tensions—for a while. But unless you resolve the deeper issues of why you're so driven to perform for others, and do some genuine soul-searching with your spouse about the effects of your drivenness on your family life, you'll probably re-create the same circumstances that you left. In fact, you may feel even more enslaved because you may prove to be your own worst boss.

More Than a Change of Scenery

At-home moms can fall into the same trap. If you show any level of competency at all, you'll probably be asked to take on major responsibilities with any volunteer organization in which you've expressed even a faint interest. Becoming heavily involved in church work alone can be a full-time (albeit nonpaying) job. The needs are constant, immediate, and heart wrenching.

Home workers face pressures from both sides, corporate and community. It can be difficult to limit your time at work, especially if you're starting or growing a small business. And some of the reasons why you decided to work from home—closer contact with your children, more time for church ministry—can quickly translate into guilt-inducing "shoulds."

Because I've written a book on children's museums, I'm a prime target when it's time to recruit chaperones for school field trips. My kids want to show off their mom's knowledge with local museums (and wheedle some pocket money for the gift shop, too). The teachers figure that at least my group won't get lost. And I really do enjoy getting to know some of my children's classmates, teachers, and the other parents along on the trip. It almost makes up for the miserable experience of riding in a school bus for an hour each way. But chaperoning a field trip consumes an entire day. I've had to limit my excursions to one per child, per year.

What Touches Your Heart?

Considering the difference between satisfaction and fulfillment will help you differentiate the results of work and investing in more eternal things.

The proper emotional response to a job well done is satisfaction. You've put out a good effort, solved a problem, completed a project, filled a client's need at a fair price, and made some money that will provide for your family. Volunteer work can also yield satisfaction; it feels good to be part of the winning team when your son's Cub Scout troop raises enough money to cover the cost of summer camp.

Fulfillment comes from a different wellspring. Fulfillment is the peace of mind that comes from knowing what your priorities are and sticking to them. It's the peace that comes from spending time with God and knowing that the rest of the day will be better for it. It's serving your kids bread hot from the oven on a rainy, gray November afternoon and hearing them pour out the details of their days at school. It's choosing to invest emotionally and spiritually in things eternal rather than things that will wither in a day or a week or a year. It's resisting the world's siren call that position and prestige, perks and paychecks are what count.

You'll find fulfillment in the work God has cut out for you, not in what someone else cuts out for you.

The Balancing Act

Another commonly cited motivation for working long hours away from home is the need for adult companionship and conversation. "I'd go nuts being cooped up all day at home playing patty-cake" is the recurring theme.

It's possible that a general feeling of discontent is a symptom of deeper issues. If you're frustrated with endless rounds of diapers and baby talk and just want to get out of the house, consider all the alternatives open to you. Perhaps going back to a full-time job, with financial need as the ostensible reason, is actually an avoidance tactic.

Is God calling you to start a neighborhood Bible study? Are you and your spouse arguing over financial priorities, and it seems that more money would solve the problem? (Maybe it would, and maybe it wouldn't.) Do you feel guilty because your parents worked hard to pay your college tuition and now you're "wasting your education" by making your young family your first priority?

If you're not quite sure why you feel compelled to take on a full-time job, ask yourself: What problems or frustrations will be solved by my working? How will working solve them? How will I know when the problem has been solved or my concerns sufficiently addressed?

A parallel to the "I'll be a better person" rationale for out-of-home-work is the fallacy that children are actually better off—more independent, self-sufficient, and happier—when both parents work full time. I doubt that many people consider their children's supposed maturity as a primary reason for working in the corporate world full time, but it certainly is a handy justification for doing what you want to do anyway.

Independence, responsibility, resourcefulness—these are important qualities that most of us want our children to develop. But these are qualities that can't be taught in absentia. If anything, parental commitment to developing children's characters argues for more time with them, not less. In fact, seeing a parent working from home—applying self-discipline and reaping the rewards of hard work and faith in God—can be a powerful example to children.

Character-building by Example

In 1990, Ruth and Jerry created a catalog dedicated to storage units and related supplies for compact discs and cassette tapes. They placed short classified ads in music magazines that targeted their market, made up their catalogs, and established relationships with their suppliers. Then they waited.

"It had been going for a year and nothing was happening," says Ruth. "In June 1991, the kids and I started praying for the business."

Several months after Ruth and the three children began each day asking for a blessing on the catalog business, one of the major storage unit manufacturers abruptly quit filling consumer orders directly. Instead, the company started referring all consumer inquiries to Ruth and Jerry's catalog. Because Ruth and Jerry had a toll-free phone line already established (Ruth picks it up in her kitchen), it was a seamless transition for customers.

"It was a direct result of prayer," says Ruth.

The kids, ages fifteen, twelve, and five, were impressed. Their enthusiasm for working for their parents on catalog-related chores was renewed.

"They still complain sometimes when we make catalogs on the kitchen table," says Ruth. "But it's been a special time because we've all worked together. Besides, they get paid for it."

In addition to assembling the catalogs, Ruth's teenage son sometimes answers the phone and takes orders; her twelve year old keeps the inventory area picked up; and her kindergartner loves to operate the credit card machine.

Ruth and Jerry's kids are learning about more than how to pitch some products. They're seeing how their parents treat customers fairly and honestly. They're seeing the results of teamwork, even with siblings. Most importantly, they're seeing a direct link between their family's efforts and faith and God's provision.

More Time for What?

To be sure, home life is very intimate and at times can seem to close in on you. There is no escape from the complete dependency imposed by a newborn. Toddlers are notorious for clinging. It's easy to think that school-aged children, just because they are able to communicate more clearly than their younger siblings, are "launched" and don't need us. The fact is, investing in people takes time. The idea that a few shreds of "quality time" can make up for a week's worth of rushed bedtimes and hurried breakfasts is simply a lie. Children and spouses need quantity time, too.

A recent survey conducted by *Working Mother* magazine of its readers revealed that 44 percent of the respondents wished they had more time with their kids. Forty percent of mothers with school-age children said they felt "very guilty" that they aren't home when the kids get out of school. Thirty percent felt guilty about not spending enough private time with their husbands.

Full-time work away from home does not make issues of communication or life satisfaction easier, but more complicated. The key is to find the balance that reflects eternal priorities. It's crucial for both spouses to sit down together and discuss long-term financial and spiritual priorities; child-rearing philosophies; and spiritual, emotional, and personal goals.

This is not pie-in-the-sky daydreaming. Setting objectives for your family will establish the framework in which other, more immediate decisions are made. As you refine your priorities and experiment with the resulting decisions, you'll begin to get an intuitive feel for the balance and rhythm that God wants to impart to your family's everyday life.

Many factors will figure in your considerations of where work fits into your family life. Keep in mind that those factors do not necessarily propel you into a single solution.

For instance, when my husband and I evaluated our financial situation while awaiting the birth of our first baby, the $125-a-month-for-ten-years student loan repayment was heavy on our minds. I felt a great deal of personal responsibility to cover that debt; we had taken it on to further my education, so I felt that my efforts should pay it back. However, the monthly bill was motivating, not guilt inducing. I felt that covering that bill was a minimum responsibility.

My commitment to paying that bill did not in any way compromise our view that it was of paramount importance that I stay home to be with our new baby. Possible solutions included part-time work or free-lancing. We decided that though I could make more money more quickly by taking on a part-time job, we instead would invest time and effort toward the long-term goal of building a free-lance career.

Agree before You Commit

Each spouse needs to be invested in the other's career decisions. The spouse who says, "I don't care what decision you make as long as you're happy" is abdicating his or her responsibility for the family's good health. He or she is probably sowing seeds of distrust, disappointment, and anger that will crop up later when tensions are high.

Mutual decision making results in mutual responsibility. The same is true when the family is facing legitimate financial pressures; it's incumbent on both spouses to fully explore all the income-enhancing options open to them. Automatically eliminating one possibility ("How dare you suggest that I go to work!") is closing the door on solutions that God may have available to you.

As you clarify the big picture, different parts of it will come into focus as well. It's like working a jigsaw puzzle from the outside edges in. Once you've got the frame completed, you know that all the remaining pieces will fit inside—somehow. (If you have leftover pieces, they must belong to another puzzle!) The daily decisions will be much easier to make once you've established your goals and priorities.

You can expect that God will regularly test you on this. Sometimes He'll present you with new opportunities that force you to reexamine your current goals and possibly readjust them, eliminating some things to accommodate new goals.

Other times, you may have to make hard choices on faith. We faced such a time in January 1989. The reins of leadership at *Crain's Chicago Business* had just passed from one editor with whom I enjoyed working to another with whom I shared an equally good relationship. Our third child was due at the end of the month, and I had been praying all fall that I'd get a big project to pull in enough money to pay some remodeling bills that would come in while I was taking my six-week maternity leave.

On Monday, January 9, my editor called. A full-time associate editor spot had just opened up—was I interested? To tell the truth, it sounded good. I'd just finished writing my first book, and I'd loved being immersed in the project, working on it nearly full time for two months. For the first time since I'd started free-lancing, I was feeling some cabin fever about working from home all the time. And those bills were coming up. Of course, I turned it down. (My editor wasn't surprised—we'd had the same conversation twice before in prior years.)

The next day I got a call from a friend at a public relations agency. I don't do PR work often, but they were in a pinch—they had to have an article ghostwritten by the end of the week. Best of all, they would pay me for the exact amount I'd been praying for—enough to cover much of the remodeling bills. The only caveat was that my friend was concerned that I get the work done before the baby came.

"No problem," I assured her. "The baby's not due for two more weeks, and I'll finish the story by Friday."

The following day, Wednesday, I researched and wrote for hours. Around midnight I began to feel the familiar pangs of labor. I got up and wrote for three more hours (breathe, type, breathe, type). On Thursday, I delivered Elizabeth at 8:18 A.M., and Mark delivered the story to the client at 3:00 P.M.

Is it a coincidence that this project came in the day after I reaffirmed my commitment to continue free-lancing from home? I don't think so.

Whistling While You Work

Like Posy, I like what I do. I'm sure that she could no sooner turn off all her ideas for crafts than I could refrain from telling people about interesting ideas, things, and people. The ideal, of course, is for all of us to work at something we enjoy and get results from our work that contribute to our self-confidence.

This is particularly important when you're considering working from home. When your work life is so closely entwined with your family life, strong feelings that you have about one will inevitably spill over to the other. There is no half-hour commute on the anonymous train or highway to cushion your family from your feelings about a frustrating day. It's easy to say "leave your work behind when you shut the door," but that's not easy to do. Particularly when you are starting out, your work situation will be on your mind a great deal. You will be mulling over your latest project while you're folding the laundry or mowing the lawn.

This is not necessarily bad. I frequently enjoy tackling some minor domestic chore when I need a break from an intense project. Doing something with my hands somehow helps my head to clear, and I can dive back into the project with some fresh thoughts. Other home workers schedule mental down-time breaks around certain daily events, such as taking a child to preschool or the arrival of the mail.

Ministry or Mayhem?

It's important to consider how your work will mesh or conflict with the ministry or calling you feel God has put on your life. Ideally, ministry and secular work reinforce each other. Perhaps you'll find it fulfilling to earn enough to give a substantial amount to a mission or other project you want to support. Or you may choose to forgo a heavier work schedule so that you will have time to devote to ministry.

At a frustrating or unproductive time in your career, you may find that God is pulling you away somewhat to focus on a spiritual breakthrough of some sort. Contributing to a ministry through time, effort, and relationships can help carry you through some dry times at work, and vice versa.

I've found that my attitude toward unexpected requests from fellow church members is a good barometer of whether or not my attitude about work is where it should be. One day I thought that I absolutely had to get to a certain point on a project. Instead, I ended up making quiche lorraine and lemon bars for two church families. One had just brought a premature baby home from the hospital; the other family's mother was bedridden due to threatened premature labor.

When my schedule is too tight to be able to respond when I want to, that tells me that I've got to make some adjustments. Sometimes that means that dinner is pulled from the freezer for a few nights running while I finish up a period of heavy work. Other times, I know that I've taken on too much, and decide to schedule a lighter load as soon as the current commitments are completed.

When you're experiencing role collision, it's especially important that your lines of communication with your spouse and children are open. Isn't it uncanny how kids pick up on our stress levels and choose that exact time to launch a major whining crusade? The week when you've got a work crunch is the week that your third grader will announce that he has a science project due in two days—and he hasn't started it yet. Then your teenager will inform you that the phys ed teacher is requiring absolutely everyone, no exceptions, to get a different uniform for an upcoming unit on gymnastics.

It's hard to respond graciously to extra demands when you're already feeling overloaded. This is when the rubber meets the road, and you'll all have to work together to decide what really needs to get done "right now" and what doesn't. It will be easier to settle on the specifics if you and your spouse are of one mind about your work situation.

Being at home affords flexibility, but location isn't the only factor you're dealing with. Deadlines and customers factor in too. Try to do a little contingency planning ahead of time so that when the crunch times come, you and your spouse will be able to cover all the bases. And make sure that you schedule some family relaxing time as soon as the pressure's off. It's important that the kids and your spouse know you appreciate their support.

The same magazine survey that underscored the amount of guilt that working mothers feel also outlined some of the ingredients for a successful work/family balance. Cooperative spouses, sympathetic employers, and jobs with a high level of personal satisfaction were listed as key factors.

If you're not sure what God is calling you to do in His kingdom, keep praying about it and studying the Scriptures. Examine your long-term ideas and dreams for your life to see how God may be speaking to you through the desires He has already planted in your heart. As you're defining your personal vision statement, examine your career-related skills, preferences, and talents. These are not mutually exclusive with the ministry God has for you!

Equipped to Serve

As you're weighing all of this, remember that there will be times when career and ministry seem to be in conflict. It will take self-discipline to keep your eternal priorities in focus, especially when they seem to be in direct conflict.

Since 1988, I've been leading a pro-life prayer meeting in my house twice a month. Each meeting consumes an entire morning. It's a rare meeting that doesn't coincide with some unexpected work crisis. It may be that the day before has been particularly unproductive, with lots of effort yielding little. Or (my personal favorite) maybe I'm experiencing a technical breakdown of one of the machines that I take for granted—the computer, fax, copier, or phone. Maybe I've just found out that I'm going to lose a day later in the week due to an impending emergency. Or maybe I just feel particularly stressed.

At any rate, the morning of prayer generally ends up feeling like a significant sacrifice. But that's just what it is—a sacrifice of time and will. I simply won't put aside this aspect of God's greater calling on my life for a temporary circumstance. This is what I'm telling the Lord as I quickly pick up the living room, usually while the first members of the group are coming up the front steps.

"You know all the things I've got to get done, and how much this time could help," is my prayer. "This is more important. I don't know what lives may be touched or saved by our intercession this morning, but I believe that there will be results because we are praying, and so I trust You to straighten out the work stuff in the meantime."

This is a very effective prayer. Not once have I regretted spending the time in the meeting. Not once has the Lord failed to relieve the tension I was feeling and take care of the crisis. Calls are miraculously returned from hard-to-reach sources. Computers heal themselves (and we all know that takes supernatural power). The capricious editor decides that the story isn't really needed until the following week, giving me extra time.

The Payoff

The main reason most people work is for the money. It's indisputable that the economic pressures on today's families force most to make some tough choices. According to the Tax Foundation, a typical family with an annual income of $53,984 sees 39.7 percent of that money siphoned off by federal, state, and local taxes. Cash income is not the only consideration. Many families find themselves boxed in by escalating health care costs. If one spouse is self-employed or feels that his or her job is threatened, the other may feel obliged to stay in an unsatisfactory job situation to ensure the family's protection with medical, dental, and other coverage.

Some financial considerations *are* set in concrete. It's just not smart to forfeit benefit coverage. Establishing savings funds for emergencies, planned spending (like vacations and college tuition), and retirement is a basic tenet of sound financial planning.

However, you probably have more flexibility than you think. A recent Labor Department survey revealed that the typical two-career family loses a half to two-thirds of its second income to the extra expenses incurred by having the second wage earner outside the home. When taxes are taken into account, the typical middle-class household ends up with only 17 percent more cash to spend by having both spouses work; an upper-income family, only 5 percent more.

First, consider the hidden costs of having a second spouse work. Day care can run from $75 to $125 per week per child. That doesn't disappear when the children enter school; you'll still have to cover before-and-after school care, plus enrichment programs like sports, art lessons, and summer camp.

Most full-time working mothers rely on some kind of household help. Maid service runs up to ninety dollars for a full day. Career clothes are no small consideration, particularly if you are in a high visibility position like sales or banking. The daily commute takes its toll, both emotionally and in terms of gas and parking. In many cases, each spouse needs his or her own car. Extra payments plus maintenance and insurance are a direct deduction against family income.

Incidentals aren't so incidental. Dry cleaning, laundry service for shirts, convenience foods, and eating out can add hundreds of dollars to a family's monthly expenses. Then there's stress spending—the "I work hard and I deserve this little treat" category. How much that treat costs depends on your particular weaknesses. The weekly pint of premium ice cream is an affordable luxury, but a monthly indulgence at a shoe salon may not be.

Stress spending also erupts in other areas. If you're too wiped out to take the kids to the library well in advance of a school project, you may end up buying an expensive set of encyclopedias so they can do research at home. You may feel that they need to dress to a certain level when they're "in public" at the day-care center. A regular lawn service, home grocery delivery, buying Christmas gifts at full price through catalogs instead of shopping local sales—such conveniences shrink your actual disposable income.

Being Home Isn't Free

When you work from home, you don't necessarily eliminate all of these expenses. After all, you are still working, and accommodation must be made for that in the budget. But working from home will give you much more leeway in choosing which items you're willing to cut back on. For instance, if you see clients once a week instead of every day, you can probably get by with three or four suits and a couple of tailored dresses, instead of a dozen suits and a dozen dresses. And the less you wear your clothes, the less you have to clean them.

You may not want to turn into an earth mom, weeding your vegetable garden while you're wrapping up a multimillion deal on your cellular phone. But you will be able to choose if you want to make a monthly run to an out-of-the-way warehouse or bulk-buy store to stock up on household staples.

Ultimately, then, it boils down to this: can you afford to work full time? Can you afford to work at home?

First, figure out your basic monthly expenses. (You'll find simple worksheets at the end of this book.) Add up your tithe; mortgage or rent; utilities; car payments; insurance premiums; car payments, maintenance, insurance, and gas; grocery bill; clothing allowance; and savings fund. Make additional lines for miscellaneous items such as a vacation fund, gifts, hobby expenses, and entertainment if those are actual expenses.

If you're currently working full time and paying for child care, start another list. Put down child care, the commuting expenses for the second spouse, extra clothes allowance, eating out and convenience foods, household help, and miscellaneous expenses like chipping in for office parties and company-mandated charitable giving. If stress spending has been a problem, be honest and add in a typical month's indulgence.

Next, dig out your pay stubs. How much money does each of you take home each month? Subtract your "cost of second job" expenses from the second income. The number you have left is how much the second wage earner is actually making. (Out of curiosity, you might divide your actual wage by the number of hours you work each month; add commuting time if you want to. Minimum wage is $4.25. Are you making that much? Many second earners are shocked to find that they don't.)

The Hidden Benefits

Dig out the employee benefits handbook from the company employing the spouse who will remain in full-time work. Scrutinize it to see how the flexible spending accounts and cafeteria benefits can help ease the transition and stretch your dollars. For instance, if you've relied on the dental plan of the spouse who's considering coming home, perhaps that can be offset by increasing the pretax set-aside money in the flexible spending account. Try to estimate your annual expenditures on routine dental care and request that that amount be set aside in the fund each month.

Here comes the hard part. With your spouse, figure out the lifestyle changes that you'd actually be willing to make so that you can afford to switch to a work-from-home position. (For purposes of discussion, I'm assuming that you'll be working twenty to thirty hours a week from home.)

Are you willing to give up the lawn service and fertilize, cut, and weed your lawn yourself? How will your wardrobe change? If one of your work-from-home goals is to spend more time with your children, will you channel that into taking them to free museums and special events to offset the fact that you pulled them out of day care or preschool?

Choose your economies. I will give up my twice-monthly cleaning lady only if we are on the brink of bankruptcy. However, the seven dollars a week it would cost to have my husband's white shirts cleaned, starched, and pressed by a commercial laundry isn't worth it to me. I actually like to iron (it's immediate gratification!), and dropping off and picking up the shirts would just be one more errand. For me, sending out the shirts is a false economy.

These choices can seem easy on paper, but weigh them carefully. You won't get any more hours in a day than you had before. You will be able to tailor your time use to more closely fit your family's needs. Beware of loading yourself up so much with extra housework, errands, and volunteer work that you end up trying to do more than you did when you worked full time.

A Life's Work

Is all of this overwhelming?

It is a great deal to consider. Take your time. You don't have to figure it all out by tomorrow. In fact, you only have to figure out as much as you need to apply right now.

The needs of mothers of young children differ dramatically from those of a woman facing the impact on her life of her aging parents. For both, working from home or arranging a flexible work schedule may be the optimum solution. But things change. A very abbreviated work situation that's perfect when you're twenty-seven with two preschoolers may not feel challenging enough when those two are in high school. At that point, you'll be pushing to accumulate money for college tuition. You may want to increase your workload and you may welcome developing some new friendships at the same time. After your children have graduated from college and are starting families of their own, you may want to return to school. Once you've graduated, you may consult part-time so that you can spend time with your grandchildren.

Going Solo with the Kids

Approach your decision making with an open mind. No situation is ideal—that's the bad news. The good news is that it'll change if you just wait long enough. Each stage of life requires a different perspective and set of priorities.

No one knows this better than Debbie. She's a professional violinist and the mother of five children, ranging in age from kindergarten to high school. She started adjusting her expectations of family life even as she launched her career.

"I had a sense of purpose to develop some momentum even before the kids were born. I never thought of quitting," she says. "I had early aspirations of playing for the Chicago Symphony. But then I saw the dedication and time it would take. My degree was in music education, not performance. I realized I wasn't really geared for solo professional work.

"My options were to teach privately or through a school, or be a free-lance musician. There's a lot more flexibility with that kind of career for a woman than simply being in a symphony, which is a full-time job."

Debbie did play in a metropolitan symphony for several seasons before her first child was born. At that point, she started pursuing free-lance jobs more energetically, helping to form a string ensemble that's now well established. She also taught violin from home for several years when her children were small.

"In a good year, I make about eight thousand dollars. Now we can get by without it, but in the early years we couldn't. It was tough," she recalls. "Now my money goes toward things like orthodontia and Christmas presents."

These days Debbie's weekly schedule varies widely. Some of it is dictated by the repertoire of pieces she must learn and polish before the string ensemble's performances. She has to practice up to twenty hours before each concert, plus attend four three-hour rehearsals.

On "off weeks" she may practice only an hour a day and spend the balance of her time catching up on housework and errands, and spending time with her kids. The next week, she may be booked for thirty hours. Her husband takes over on the weekends when the concerts are held.

Through it all, she has practiced over and around her kids.

"I have a lot of patience. It doesn't generally bother me to sit and be interrupted. But if I'm under the gun, I tell them, 'Don't bother me, please.' It works about half the time. The other times, I have no problems about borrowing a friend's arms to take the kids or getting a sitter.

"There are times when I've put the music on the fridge with magnets and tossed Cheerios to the kids on the kitchen floor to keep them occupied while I practiced."

According to Debbie, she had to embrace the fact that she'd put herself on a "mommy track" for several years. "You have to be realistic with your expectations," she says. "Motherhood involves sacrifice. The priority is taking care of that child in the first couple of years. You may not work for a year. But you have chosen that path. Find things you can do—and don't whine. It may feel overwhelming and impossible. But a year from now, you'll be able to work things out. Look at it over the long term, not the short term."

The days when her oldest children will be leaving home are fast approaching. And for the first time in about eighteen years, Debbie soon won't have a small child at home during the day.

"Looking back, I wouldn't choose to have changed a thing," she says. "So what if I might have played in the St. Louis Symphony? The career does not take the place of those warm little kisses and hugs."

·3·

Developing Your Personal Business Plan

A T AGE TWENTY-FIVE, Kathleen is doing what she thought wouldn't come to her for another decade: she has successfully launched her own home-based interior decorating business.

Kathleen was in high school when she settled on interior design as her career. Eager to get started, she graduated early and entered an intensive twelve-month training course in lieu of pursuing the more traditional four-year college track.

At age eighteen, she started working for a furniture store in a small city. A year later, she moved to a major metropolitan furniture chain, where she immediately became the top-producing designer/salesperson for three years in a row.

"Ever since day one, it was my dream to have my own business," she says. "There I was, working on a three-and-a-half percent commission and making thirty thousand dollars a year. I saw tons of money change hands, and only a little bit stayed with me. I was doing all the selling, design, paperwork, and follow-up. I thought, Gosh, if I can do it for someone else, I can do it for myself.

"It's really scary to go out on your own. The whole reason I did it is that I wanted to stay home with my baby so badly."

So in the latter part of 1991, Kathleen started collecting all the paperwork she'd need to become self-employed. It took longer than she'd thought—six months—to get all the tax work, credentials, and other licenses required. She also had to make some ethical decisions.

"I was really careful when I left the store," she explains. "I referred current customers to other staff designers. I did tell the drapery studio that I'd be opening my own business, because I knew I'd be referring business to them."

After taking several months off when baby Bridgette Colleen arrived, Kathleen officially opened shop. She already had plenty of work waiting because some of her prior clients had tracked her down. In her first five months of operating, she grossed twenty-five thousand dollars—close to her annual earnings at the store. (Clients can choose to pay Kathleen an hourly rate for a consultation, or they can get her services free when they buy a certain amount of furnishings on which she keeps a commission from the manufacturer while still passing on a discount to the client.)

"I don't advertise. I feel that every client who comes is God's blessing," she says. "I just got home last night from a meeting with a new client with a check for ten thousand dollars. I'm doing this job because we need the money, but I also love it."

Because her income is likely to be unpredictable for the next several years, Kathleen is trying to plan carefully. In doing so, she's trying to spend what she needs to be professional, yet not box herself into a corner with unnecessary debt or too much overhead.

"If you're going to do it on your own, you can't be 'Sally home decorator.' You almost have to be overly professional," she says. So far, she has bought a word processor instead of a computer, installed two business phone lines, and spent a great deal of effort and money on her business stationery and forms.

"I have a form and a contract for everything," she emphasizes. "I can't afford to eat a twenty thousand dollar living room set because someone doesn't like it. I probably have seventy-five different forms to cover all the liabilities."

Though she runs out to the neighborhood copy center "twice a day," she's determined not to get a copier or a fax machine until more money has come in. "Anything that's not necessary we haven't invested in yet," she says. "Most things you can do without. You just have to work a little harder."

At first the baby accompanied Kathleen on her twice-monthly forays to a furniture showcase mart, where she searches for the items that her clients need. As Bridgette Colleen grows and gets more mobile, Kathleen expects to pay a neighbor to watch her during the day when she has to be away. At the same time, she intends to keep her arrangement with her husband to schedule client appointments during the evening when he can watch the baby. She does creative thinking and paperwork during her daughter's naptimes.

Somewhat to her surprise, Kathleen has found that her work has had a spiritual impact on some of her clients. "Clients ask me, 'What are you doing for the weekend?' and I'll say, 'Our church is doing this neat thing. Why don't you come?' Now two of my clients attend our church! I'm so excited about our church that it just comes up."

Kathleen is already laying the groundwork for her fledgling firm's growth. Within a couple of years, she wants to start taking on associate designers. She plans to keep her own clients, delegate some paperwork to associates, consult on their jobs, and get part of their fee. In the meantime, she has already shifted some of the financial paperwork to a home-based accountant.

It's her preference to find a Christian assistant, but she's also aware that talent and desire are crucial. "I can't hire someone who has no talent just because he or she is a Christian. My business would go to pot," she says.

Plan Your Work

It's no wonder that Kathleen is going places, even as she's staying home. Intuitively, she has in mind a personal business plan: she knows what her goals are and she's working to meet them without compromising her underlying objective, which is to rear her children herself.

As you're considering your work options, it's crucial to develop a personal business plan that outlines your family, spiritual, emotional, and financial objectives. All of these components are intertwined. Making an elaborate plan for one without considering the others will result in conflicts in how you spend your time, money, and emotional resources.

Start by listing the primary objectives for your life. For most of us, these include continuing to grow in our spiritual walk; having loving, stable marriages; rearing God-fearing children; and responding to God's call regarding the ministries He has for us.

Specific goals support those objectives. Working from home or arranging a flexible work schedule supports two objectives: spending time with your children to impart your values and earning money to provide for the family. Setting and achieving certain financial goals for retirement contributes to a stable marriage. Installing a state-of-the-art word processing system that helps the swamped church secretary is harnessing work skills for the Kingdom. From your objectives, develop your goals.

Developing an Entrepreneurial Mindset

Goals are not of much use without an overall plan. Achieving a goal for its own sake is like taking a tour of dead-end streets. It may be a pleasant drive, but if it doesn't get you anywhere, what's the point? That's why it's so important to narrow down your goals from your life objectives. You can reach those objectives from any number of angles, but you will probably be most successful building on the strengths and experiences that you already possess.

It's not enough any more to have a single career skill used over and over the same way. The marketplace is changing rapidly, with expectations of job stability shifting from day to day, from industry to industry.

Take the initiative to stay a step ahead of those changes to stay on track with your overall objectives. The old assumptions about working hard and getting regular promotions and raises along a narrow career track are largely passé. Add that to the fact that your own life will continue to change, and you can see how important it is to be adept at anticipating and responding to changing circumstances.

If you're self-employed, you'll be selling your services or products to clients or to the public. You'll need to be good at reading the marketplace to adapt your services or products to stay in business.

If you're going to try to translate a traditional corporate position to an alternative work track either at home or at the office, you'll need to have a persuasive set of arguments as to why this is beneficial to your employer. You'll need to keep abreast of changes in the company so that you can continue to be valuable as an alternative schedule worker—and your job performance must reflect your value to the organization.

Take It Personally

I call this process building a personal business plan. A traditional business plan outlines a new company's objectives, lists the steps that the entrepreneur intends to take to get there, and includes measures of success. Usually the key turning point is when the start-up company begins to make a profit. That's when the founders and investors start to reap the benefits of their efforts.

You also will know when you're on the right track toward achieving your objectives when you start to "turn a profit." Some of your profits will be in the usual sense—income that provides for your family. However, other profits will be intangible.

One of my "profits" is having the time to develop long-term support relationships with women in crisis pregnancy. To me, nothing is richer than seeing a new baby whose mother has weathered some tough circumstances and has come through stronger due to prayer and loving support.

Just as entrepreneurs look at numerous routes to success, so you also need to consider the various methods by which you can achieve your objectives. Take an inventory of your skills, abilities, talents, and experience.

Start with your educational and work accomplishments—they're easiest to quantify. Step outside your job description or résumé to define your work abilities in terms of skill sets. For instance, if you're an administrative assistant to a corporate executive, you're probably used to coordinating special projects. In order to do that, you work with other employees to collect the appropriate information on time, get it organized into the proper format, and get it reviewed by other staff members so that everyone agrees with the report's conclusions. The skills involved to get the job done are: research, word processing/formatting, and consensus building.

Each of these skills can be applied to different situations—even those where an administrative assistant seemingly "need not apply." For instance, starting a business as a wedding coordinator requires many of the same abilities. You need to pull together disparate bits of information into a coherent whole (research and formatting) and get the bride and her entourage to agree on details like colors, dresses, flowers, and so on (consensus building). And what is more deadline-oriented than a wedding? Looking at your abilities in terms of skill sets can help you see how they transfer to different work settings.

If you are a professional or "knowledge-based worker" who tends to view job security in terms of individual abilities instead of organizational structure, you may already be feeling dissatisfied within a traditional corporation. Similarly, if you're an "idea person" in a company whose culture doesn't recognize or reward "intrapreneurship," or innovation from within, you're probably frustrated. Try to pinpoint the cause of your negative feelings. Maybe you're more than ready to go out on your own.

Don't forget to include work-related training or adult and continuing education courses you've taken. Mastery of a much-in-demand word processing or computer graphics program can be the foundation for your self-employment.

Look at church work and other interests at which you're highly skilled. Try to discern exactly what appeals to you about these activities. When you lead a youth fellowship group, what do you like most? "Working with the kids" is not specific enough. Do you like discipling one or two up-and-coming leaders, helping them grow spiritually and personally, or is it the planning of the big meetings and parties that you enjoy most? Maybe you thrive on enhancing personal communication—helping a father and son resolve their differences over the son's proposed college plans.

Turning Your Inside Experience Out

Diana has waded through many of these issues.

Until her first daughter, now eleven, was three years old, Diana worked full-time for an international computer software development company as a systems analyst. "I was always an entrepreneur at the company," she recalls. "I developed a training class for them for which they charged outside clients five hundred dollars per student."

Though she had what many people would consider an ideal arrangement (her daughter was in child care nearby and Diana nursed her during her lunch hours), the separation proved too stressful. Convinced because of her "intrapreneurship" that she could be a successful entrepreneur, Diana quit her job. She perceived that at home she'd actually have more opportunity for intellectual stimulation pursuing her own ideas.

"I'm curious. I'm never bored. Most of a job is routine—it's boring," she says.

Another attitude that Diana has had from the start is that "you don't have to a build a multi-billion-dollar business to be successful.

Because something lasts for five or ten years doesn't mean it's not successful. If it was good, then it was successful."

She started distributing a line of natural vitamins and other household supplies. Though it never developed into a full-fledged business, it did bolster her confidence in her ability to sell. "I found out that you have to be persistent in sales. Typically, you don't get a sale in the first contact. You have to contact people over and over," she says.

One Stitch at a Time

With tuition for her daughters' Christian school an ongoing financial pressure, Diana took another calculated risk. For years, she'd been teaching sewing classes at a local store. In the process, she'd been looking for a thorough, nontechnical how-to book for serger sewing machines. (Sergers duplicate factory sewing techniques for home use.)

"I found that the books on the market didn't meet the needs of my students," she says. "I had [the book] in the computer and kept revising it. And of course one of the basics of business is that you know the customer and the needs of your customer, and fill those needs."

So she wrote and illustrated a guide to the machines and has been selling it through sewing retailers and mail-order catalogs. "I think it's important to try different things and see what works," she says. "I've been teaching and writing and sewing on a serger for years, and just now all of them have come together."

Diana ordered two thousand copies of the book for the first printing. She could have cut the cost of each copy by ordering a larger print run initially, but she felt it wasn't prudent to tie up so much money in inventory. So far, the twenty-five dollar guide has received excellent reviews from sewing magazines. About half of the first printing has been sold, and already Diana has turned a profit on the project. She's now at work on a less extensive, less expensive beginner's guide to the machines.

"I wanted a niche that's small enough to own but big enough to keep me alive. I'll work this niche for a while," says Diana, adding that she has ideas for other books not related to sewing. "I feel that it really complements my family. While I'm working on the books, my five year old can sit in my lap.

"I'm trusting in God. My feeling is that God will provide for us if we are open to His guidance. Maybe publishing will give us personal growth and the income to support us as well."

Defeating the Fear of Fear

There are only two things to be afraid of when you're thinking of going out on your own: failure and success. When you have a clear sense of what your long-term objectives are, you don't have to be overwhelmed by either one, as Diana's experience shows. She has been willing to experiment with several different ventures, integrating her experiences into new trials. Not everything she has tried has been a blockbuster, but she hasn't wasted any of her experience.

Without dwelling too long on a list of scary scenarios, here's a look at the potential consequences of both extremes. Let's get the bad news out of the way first. What happens if you start a business or try being self-employed—and you've completely misread the market? You've certainly lost time, and possibly some money (more on that in chapter 9). Maybe worse, you may feel your confidence eroded. There may be marital or family stresses as you try to deal with ensuing financial pressures. You may feel panicky and forced to quickly get a "regular job" to restore life back to normal. It's embarrassing to answer the well-meaning but ill-timed inquiries of family and friends who want to know how it's going.

Let me assure you from personal experience: failure is disappointing. It hurts. But whether or not it's devastating is up to you.

When the Rubber Met the Road—and Left Skid Marks

In the spring of 1991, I introduced a Midwest family travel newsletter. I'd done everything I was supposed to—researched the market, examined travel trends, and analyzed the competition. I was sure that because my travel books had sold respectably well, and because the Midwest is frequently overlooked by travel writers, that there was plenty of latent demand for a newsletter on places to go and things to do with kids. Further, I rather overconfidently believed that because I'd been reporting on businesses I knew enough to run one.

I was right about one thing: I'm a good travel writer. The newsletter got excellent publicity. Travel editors thought it was great. However, I made a very expensive mistake with a small advertising agency that I'd hired for a direct marketing push. They sent the newsletters to the wrong market segment—and because I'd neglected to specify, in writing, every detail of the mailing plan, they refused responsibility. I was out six thousand dollars—a big chunk of the money I'd allotted to my introductory direct-mail splash.

I'd also underestimated the amount of work it takes to keep on top of the administrative details—subscription fulfillment, renewals, billing, collecting, processing credit card orders, gift subscriptions—egad! So much for superwoman. The last straw came in the spring of 1992, when I abruptly became quite ill. For two months I couldn't work on the newsletter or anything else. Finally I realized that something had to go. Reluctantly, I published one last issue and refunded the balance due to my patient subscribers.

Oh—and my whole family started to pray. I was still convinced that the newsletter filled a need. My husband and I hoped, and we all fervently prayed every night, that someone would buy it and carry on.

This story will continue in a minute. The point is that apparent failure didn't kill me. Not everything works out, even when you do everything just as you're supposed to (which I hadn't, ignoring my own advice!).

I had lots of noble goals for the newsletter. I wanted to equip parents with ideas for wholesome family activities. I wanted to run my own business so that I could have even more control over my time. I also wanted to get experience in administration and financial management so that I'd be prepared to be an effective director of a nonprofit organization. Surely, with all those wonderful objectives, God would bless me. Wouldn't He?

Apparently not. The future was looking very gray. Telling my friends and family that I was suspending publication was painful. To purchase some expensive computer equipment and cover some operating expenses, I'd taken out an eighteen thousand dollar bank loan. I was glad I had the equipment, but we figured it would take two full years to pay back the loan. I cringed when I saw how hard my husband had to work to make up for my lost income, which had been poured into the newsletter. That, plus lingering effects of the illness, pushed me to the brink of depression.

But God was not done with that newsletter yet.

After several stalled inquiries, someone showed interest in buying it. Unbeknownst to me, a long-time free-lance friend had teamed up with a local investor to start a newsletter publishing company. During one of our semiannual lunch dates, she told me all about the new company. Their first product was a specialized legal reporting newsletter. Their second was my travel newsletter. In November 1992, it was acquired by Rubber Meets the Road Publishing. After all those months of praying, God had heard us! I was so relieved I cried.

The new owners asked me to stay on as editor for some time. Besides being paid for what I'd previously been doing for nothing, I had a budget for research, travel expenses, and a part-time editorial assistant. For whatever reason, the Lord didn't want me to be running a company. That's okay by me.

Fear of Success

The other great entrepreneurial fear is of success. Usually this is not as realistic a fear as that of failure. Statistically speaking, more small businesses fail than become long-term success stories. However, one common reason why fledgling companies close is that they are victims of their own initial success. The owners, flush with excitement when their first product or service gets a rush of customers, expand too quickly. Suddenly they can't adequately serve their old customers, never mind the new ones. Apprehension about getting in over your head, having your life taken over by your business, stress on your marriage and family, pressure to take on investors or get additional funding, or other fallout of overnight success can be paralyzing.

Fear of failure and fear of success: neither is fatal, especially if you are aware that you're afraid. Instead of focusing on the fear, channel your energy into tracking your progress. Agree with your spouse on "bailout triggers." For instance, agree to invest a certain amount of time and money in the venture for a certain period of time. If you're not getting encouraging results by the time the deadline rolls around, reevaluate. See what you need to change. Are your original assumptions holding up? Is there really a market for your service or product?

If early success is the problem, seek out the advice of entrepreneurs who are a few steps ahead of you. Don't believe in success itself—try to find out exactly why people are buying. Resist the urge to buy expensive equipment until you're sure that your strong start will continue.

Figure out what responsibilities you want to delegate and which ones you want to keep doing. Would you rather manage the whole thing and delegate the actual work (including the parts you like)? Or would you rather hire someone to manage your less-favorite parts and keep on selling, buying, writing, or doing whatever you're best at? See if your spouse or older children can take over some of the responsibilities of the company. And count your blessings!

Homeward Bound or Outward Bound?

Once you've clarified your life objectives and outlined some of the goals that support those objectives, consider the kind of work style that you want. Do you hope to get or make a position that's home-based so that you can spend more time with young children or aging parents? Is your main desire flexibility, so that you are willing to work unpredictable hours or seasons and be relatively free at other times? Are you the primary or sole breadwinner for the family, yet you want a position that still allows for a significant amount of time at home?

Your home business may be sparked by an idea or item that you love but that entails work that you don't care for. Think about the work you'll be doing—not just about the end product. You may fall in love with an item you love and that you're convinced will be in demand. Perhaps mail-order is a good vehicle for selling it, but if you hate order taking, invoicing, packing, and other administrative necessities, you'll soon grow to detest the sight of the cute thing you were so enthusiastic about.

Division of labor along their work preferences is one reason why Ruth and Jerry are enjoying the process of starting their mail-order business. "I love all the paperwork. I hate negotiating. Jerry loves to negotiate [with suppliers]," says Ruth. Jerry also writes the copy for the catalog and is in charge of its illustration and design.

Not all people are cut out for work at home. Mainly, this is a matter of personal work style. Some folks thrive on the synergy of the office. They are much more productive when they know that they have to give a progress report on a certain project to senior management by 2:00 P.M. on Thursday.

But my research leads me to believe that the greatest predicator of success in the work-from-home life-style is the strength of your desire.

How Badly Do You Want It?

It's easy to say that introverts are made for working from home because they don't mind the isolation. A strongly motivated extrovert, though, will adapt. (I'm living proof.) In fact, you could argue that an extrovert will be more successful because he or she won't have to overcome internal barriers and inertia to get out there and network and sell. Introverts can be all too content to hide out at home.

If working from home appears to fit with your objectives and goals, do some self-analysis to discern which of your personality strengths and work environment preferences will enhance your chances of success. Likewise, when you discover something that doesn't seem to mesh with working from home, think about how you can compensate for it, change it, or work around it.

A helpful aid in pinpointing your preferences is the DiSC test. Your gut response to a set of adjectives results in a profile of your preferences in personal interaction, including the types of situations that you do best in and those in which you're likely to be uncomfortable. For instance, you won't find out merely that you like people, but that, say, people find you inspirational—an asset in sales; however, you need to be more detail-oriented to boost credibility. (Information on ordering the self-administered test is found in chapter 10.)

Here are some other factors to consider. Do you prefer:

Group projects	or	individual projects?
Social interaction at work	or	maximum time efficiency?
The "unwind" time provided by a commute, which serves to keep work and home separate	or	do you find yourself running personal errands during work, blending personal and home business?
Do you see your home as a refuge from the outside world	or	do you see your home as a base for all kinds of projects?

Is it hard for you to leave unfinished projects on your desk at the end of the work day	or	can you walk away from an in-process project, putting it "on hold" mentally?
Do you enjoy the process	or	the product of work more?
Do you prefer to give your children undivided attention when they're with you and then be totally free to concentrate on your task	or	do you think it's reasonable to expect children to amuse themselves while you're focusing on a project nearby?
Do you prefer predictability	or	the unexpected?
Do you love meetings and group brainstorming	or	do you think that meetings are usually a waste of time; you prefer one-on-one interaction?
Do you procrastinate	or	do you find it relatively easy to set priorities for a project or the week and stick to them?
Do you have a low tolerance for interruptions at work	or	are you able to maintain several trains of thought at once?
Do you frequently regret having said yes to "extra" commitments, such as volunteer or extended family commitments	or	have you chosen a few categories of commitments that you're willing to participate in (and does your spouse back you up when you decline other requests?)

Do you prefer a predictable routine	or	a day full of challenges and goals to be met?
Do you find that deadline work makes you more efficient and improves quality	or	do you tend to react to deadline pressure by lowering quality to "get this out of my hair"?
Would you rather have a job with higher pay but lower prestige	or	would you prefer a job with high visibility and prestige but less pay?
Are you willing to master new technologies	or	are you intimidated by high-tech tools, even if you know they'll help you be more productive?
Does it embarrass you to ask others for advice and help	or	are you willing to swallow your pride and take others' recommendations?

Be honest with yourself as you review your strengths, weaknesses, and preferences. Just because you have strong preferences in your work style, situation, or environment doesn't mean that you can't change. Please don't see these personal skills and preferences inventories as set in concrete. Think about how your tolerance for noise, clutter, and interrupted thought has increased since you became a parent!

How's Your Follow-through?

Keep in mind, though, that there is one criterion for successful home workers. They are not only self-starters; they are finishers as well. One key to working from home is the regular exercise of self-discipline. At the same time, self-discipline must be held in balance with grace. Without grace, you become your own slave driver. Grace without self-discipline is merely an excuse to be disorganized, unfocused, and lazy. Find the balance that is right for you.

The particular demands of the job that you are considering performing from home will also shape your work life-style. The substance of some jobs can be accomplished in relative anonymity at home. Computer programming, research, and creative work, such as design and administrative support functions, are such jobs. On the other hand, some careers inherently involve lots of people contact. Most sales jobs—real estate, toys, Tupperware, or other products—are like that. In between are jobs where research and paperwork can be handled at home but a certain amount of personal interaction is a necessity, such as management consulting, teaching, counseling, social work, and training.

If you've reviewed the list above and realized that you probably function best in a traditional office environment, don't despair. We'll get into the specifics of arranging a flexible work situation in chapter eight.

As you're reviewing your preferences, try to think of corollaries in your home life. If, for instance, you determine that you'll definitely need three hours of completely uninterrupted time each day, and so you'll be putting your toddler with a baby-sitter, how will you compensate for that so that you will still be making progress toward your overall objective of spending time with him? You might make a point of taking your child "out to lunch" (at home, the park, or with friends) once or twice a week to reinforce the fact that time with him is special and something you look forward to.

As much as I like being with my children, I have very little patience for having them play at my desk. Still, when my four year old approaches me with a pile of fairy tales and the plea to "read to me, Mommy," I'll gladly set her books atop my notepads, take her on my lap, and read. Let the machine answer the phone and the story languish in the computer for just a few minutes. I'm investing in my daughter. I'm also sending her a mixed message—stay away from Mommy's desk unless you're asking her to read. At this point, I'm willing to sacrifice the sanctity of my desk for the sake of my relationship with her.

If you tend to be introverted and you're in a relatively isolating profession (such as accounting or graphic design), how will you make sure you maintain friendships? Maybe joining a weekly fellowship group or monthly prayer breakfast will fill the bill. Don't forget to count professional, association, and local business meetings into the equation so that you don't overcommit yourself. You can always add more things to your schedule, but it's hard to take things out.

The Big Sell

Corporate America is beginning to wake up to the fact that it has got to be more flexible in terms of hours and workplace to keep qualified, productive workers on board. And partly because of the multitudes of professionals and executive-level entrepreneurs who are performing at least some of their work from their home offices, home-work has become a cutting-edge trend.

Nevertheless, when you are a home-based or flexible worker, frequently you will be selling your situation along with your skills. Unabashed (not aggressive) self-promotion comes with the territory.

Part of this will be sparked by curiosity by people who wish they or their spouses worked from home. They'll freely inquire about how you got your situation and how it works out. They are already sold on the benefits of home-work. Widespread curiosity about home working is an advantage to entrepreneurs. Your enthusiasm about your work life-style can turn into a marketing advantage if it helps the potential customer remember who you are.

Clients and bosses, though, may not be as openly enthusiastic. Especially in the beginning, you may find yourself having to deliberately direct their attention to the actual job that you're doing rather than the specifics of where you get your work done. After a while, if things are progressing satisfactorily, this will probably subside. After you become more established and you are a known quantity, the issue of where you work will become neutral. Employers and clients are ultimately more interested in what you do, not where you do it.

With that said, it's still true that constant sales is an integral part of being an entrepreneur or self-employed. I used to think that because I'm a writer, I don't sell. Then it dawned on me that I'm constantly selling—my ideas, my track record, my credibility.

Kathleen sells more than tables and couches. She's also selling her taste and her interpretation of someone else's life back to them. Diana is selling her books, but also her authority as an expert on serger sewing machines. Much of her credibility is based on her years of teaching and direct contact with novice seamstresses.

"When you sell, you always want to think about the benefit and value of the product to the customer, not what it means to you.

People don't like to be 'sold,' " says Diana. "Be relaxed. You share your enthusiasms when you sell."

When you go out on your own, selling comes with the territory. You may feel uncomfortable with it at first, but as your confidence in your services and abilities grows, selling will become more natural.

Margaret's Story

Let me introduce you to my friend Margaret. In the past year, she and her husband have been weighing most of the issues discussed in this chapter.

Margaret has been out of the paid work force for about seven years—since the birth of her son, Matthew. Prior to that, she ran a graphics and publications department for the national headquarters office of a small denomination. She was in charge of producing the graphics and overseeing the printing for a variety of publications, from simple calendars and brochures to fairly complex manuals. She trained and supervised people. She even did some writing.

For the past seven years, Margaret and her husband, Darch, have been heavily involved with leading the Sunday morning children's church program at our church. They have introduced many innovative, entertaining, and spiritually rich programs for the kids. All of their combined skills have been used to the max for these productions. At home, Margaret has spent her time in domestic pursuits—gardening, hospitality, sewing, crafts, and rearing their son.

Now that Matthew is in school, Margaret and Darch are reevaluating how she spends her time.

They have some mounting financial pressures. They bought a fixer-upper house that they have not fixed up. Now it needs some major repairs, to the tune of about thirty-five thousand dollars. For the first time, they did some financial planning and were jolted by the fact that they don't have much savings for emergencies, retirement, or their son's college education. While Darch's job seems secure at the moment, his industry has gone through several shakeouts and subsequent rounds of layoffs, and more are predicted. Establishing an emergency fund and putting aside seed money for retirement and college bring the couple's medium-term financial goals to over fifty thousand dollars.

Their long-term objective is to attain a greater level of financial security. Getting their house in shape is a cornerstone of that plan.

"Finances are definitely a priority right now," says Margaret. "Our goals are becoming real motivations." To accomplish those goals, it seems clear to them that Margaret needs to start bringing in some money.

They are now tracking their spending and feel that their budget is reasonable. Margaret doesn't detect any out-of-control habits that need to be reined in before extra money comes on the scene. (When asked about stress spending, she says, "When I was working, I did buy a three hundred dollar hat once to reward myself for meeting a deadline.")

Unfortunately, Margaret has not kept abreast of the trends in her field. She is not even sure what kind of hardware and software are now being used in desktop publishing. However, she has done a few free-lance projects over the past few years. Her keyline and paste-up skills are the least rusty. (Keyline and paste-up are the process of physically laying out type, photos, and illustrations on a page.)

Margaret and Darch need to work through several issues. First, they need to decide which is more important to them: achieving their financial goals quickly, or taking a slower, more life-style-oriented approach. If making money was their only goal, Margaret could get up to speed on desktop publishing and get a job with an advertising agency, printer, or corporation.

But they are also concerned about their life-style. Margaret wants to be there when her son comes home from school. Her husband wants her to be able to continue her artistic pursuits. They both remain committed to working with the children's church program. Margaret usually does much of the preparation for that while Darch is at work. So, they have some important life-style and ministry considerations that temper their need to boost their income.

So far, Margaret has been playing around with a variety of ideas other than returning to graphic design. She has produced some funky painted sneakers for her family. Maybe she could paint sneakers and sell them at crafts fairs for twenty-five dollars and up a pair. She also has a portfolio of drawings and prints that she has done in the past several years. Perhaps she should become an illustrator. Or it's possible that her experience with children could lead to work in developing Sunday school curriculum.

Much to her credit, Margaret has zeroed in on a weakness that could cripple her if she decides to pursue a free-lance career. "If I have free-lance work that needs to be done by a deadline, I do get it done," she says. "Yet, I feel that my lack of discipline is a big enough problem that it could sabotage my success."

She is considering how much she depends on an external structure to focus her efforts. "It's really more of a scheduling structure than a workplace structure," she adds. "I want to get my artistic skills back up to par, but I'm out of touch with my inner motivation. I'm not really motivated to restart it for its own sake."

One immediate benefit to the process that Margaret and Darch are in is that they've started to really see her labor as an asset, whether it's directed to the household or in the marketplace.

What did they decide to do? We'll find out in the next chapter.

·4·

The Entrepreneurial Mindset

I F I DIDN'T have this business, I would have had to go out and get a full-time job. My kids would not only have lost their dad, they'd have lost their mom, too."

After twelve years of marriage, Rose's husband walked out on her. Through the emotional devastation of divorce and the pain of trying to create a healing home for her two daughters, she had one day-to-day constant: her home-based desktop publishing business.

Well before the marriage hit the rocks, God knew that Rose would need a lucrative skill to support her family. Unbeknownst to her, His tender Father's heart was protecting her, leading her to develop an interest and part-time career before she had an inkling that she'd be depending on it. God didn't merely react to her circumstances—He anticipated them.

"When the time came, I was equipped to bear a burden I didn't think I could handle," Rose says. "In many respects, I function as a full-time parent and have a full-time job. I have a strong commitment to my kids. But I also have to make a living."

When her two daughters, now approaching adolescence, were very young, Rose played around with computer graphics and desktop publishing technology, keeping a finger in the career that she'd once had full time. "I would never recommend that anyone do it the way I did," she says. "I had no plan at all, but I was at a nice jumping-off point when I had to focus on it."

She quickly followed up on some leads that she'd casually been developing. Gulping hard, Rose remortgaged her house to finance her business. She bought a more sophisticated computer, a light table, fax, printer, and scanner.

Her hard work—and faith in God—paid off. Her income has increased in each of the five years since she started working from home full time. Her earnings provide 75 percent of her family's income; child support accounts for the rest.

While the growth trend has been steady, the day-to-day flow of work isn't. "I have some very stable accounts, like my monthly newsletters and annual convention materials. There are times when I'm very busy. When you're up at 3:00 A.M. you have way too much time to think and not enough brain cells operating," she says. "But then a couple of months later I'll need the money [earned during the overload time]. The car will break down, and I'll know why I was so busy. Last month was very slow, but I also had a child home with a virus and stress related to the divorce. I needed the money, but I was needed somewhere else. Then this month things picked up, and now I'm back on track."

Rose says that the fact that she's home-based has been a non-issue with her clients. She meets potential and new clients in their offices; regular clients sometimes drop by her home office, but rarely.

"Once I've got a rapport and have established myself as a professional, they don't care where my office is," she says. "I always refer to my office, not my house. When I'm out, I'll just say, 'I'll be out from one o'clock to three.' They don't have to know that I'm in the second grade making a papier-maché project."

Rose is adamant about taking personal time. "A lot of people skip their vacations when they're self-employed. Personally, I plan my year around my vacation," she says. She informs her clients of her impending absence two months in advance and coordinates with another home-based graphic artist to cover any emergencies.

It's that bit of peer interaction that reminds Rose of the only thing she misses: coworkers. "It's really fun to work with someone else. I miss the exchange of ideas," she says. Once her girls are away at college, she may move her office to a small business center so she can be with people during the day. For now, involvement with her girls' school and in church projects keeps her socially active.

Eventually, Rose thinks she'd like to take some college-level business management courses and perhaps pursue a career in small business consulting. But those plans are well in the future.

"For now, I am quite content. My job has its own sufficiency for what I need, and for my family's needs. It has allowed me to be with my kids when they've needed a lot of time from me. They see their mother as someone who can pick up and go on under the most devastating circumstances.

"God doesn't promise us smooth sailing," Rose says. "When the marriage was on the wane, I realized that God is still faithful. And I have the strength to make it through some of the worst of what life can dish out."

The "You" in Working for Yourself

As Rose passed through deep waters, she clung to the eternal priorities God had already established in her life. He has more than met her faith in Him by blessing her business over and over through financial stability and good client relationships and, most importantly, through protecting her relationship with her children. What a precious example this is of the psalmist's description of God as the "father to the fatherless, a defender of widows." (Psalm 68:5)

One of Rose's greatest assets as she was plunged into her business venture was her already-budding entrepreneurial spirit. Her can-do attitude has been an important factor in the prosperity of her business. An entrepreneurial mindset is an essential factor shared by virtually all successful home workers regardless of the specifics of their situations—business owner, free-lancer, or telecommuter.

Alternative career track employees in traditional corporations also have to maintain an entrepreneurial edge. They have to take greater initiatives than "regular" employees to obtain and keep their positions. Some of the characteristics of the entrepreneurial mindset are what you'd expect: being a self-starter, being organized, and being willing to work hard. In the next section we'll look at these and at some other important traits that may seem surprising, such as being a self-stopper and being able to relax.

You Just Knew the Proverbs 31 Lady Would Turn Up Somewhere in This Book

We already have a role model of an entrepreneurial woman in the Bible, the Proverbs 31 "good wife." Sometimes it seems as though folks with socio-political agendas try to remake her to serve as a shining example of whatever their viewpoint happens to be. Without falling into that trap, we can clearly observe that she embodies several ideals that we would do well to emulate as we consider home business options.

She is a model of industry, getting up before dawn and working by lamplight into the evening. According to the New International Version, she "works with energy." Certainly, self-discipline is a keystone of home business.

She isn't afraid to invest in income-producing assets. Back in her day, a valued commodity was a vineyard. These days, it's more apropos to think in terms of the equipment essential to efficiency and quality. The principle is the same.

She's not so focused on her industry that she forgets to extend blessing to others. She treats her servant girls fairly, setting an example to us when we hire help for our business or home. And she goes out of her way to help the poor and needy. In other words, she isn't stingy with her profits. Her work isn't done until she has given as freely to others as God has given to her.

The Proverbs 31 good wife is not merely busy, she is a model of fruitfulness. Her activity is focused to bring about certain results. She is goal-oriented, but she is not a slave to her goals. In fact, the very way she goes about her work enhances her reputation (she's to be praised for her work) and that of her husband.

The Fruitful Yield

The side effects of her industry—reputation, household harmony, appreciation by her husband—underscore the difference between activity and fruitfulness. Activity is simply doing stuff. When you are rearing children and running a household, there is always something to do. (Remember that time-worn management aphorism that the work always expands to fit the allotted time?) Making it to the bottom of the to-do list with every item scratched out means that all those tasks have been completed. It does not necessarily mean that your effort has been fruitful.

In some ways, fruitfulness is the antithesis of activity. It is looking beyond the mere list of daily accomplishments to the eternal objectives. Activity does not consider the emotional and spiritual aspects of getting the job done, so long as it does get done. You can be bustling with activity and yet be counterproductive. Who among us has not bruised a child's spirit by mouthing "shut up" while we are on the phone, or waved a child away without a glance when we're concentrating on a last-minute project? (Thankfully, the damage is usually temporary, especially if we're humble enough to ask forgiveness.)

Fruitfulness also is another way to look at setting work priorities. On one day, a decision to spend some extra time getting to know a client may have long-term fruit as the relationship grows. The next day, spending a couple of hours in planning and scheduling may be sowing seeds of fruitfulness for the upcoming weeks.

Sometimes the fruitful thing will not even look energetic to the casual observer. Certainly, making regular time with the Lord is fruitful. So is making the extra effort to treat business partners, suppliers, customers, employees, and coworkers as Jesus would.

The harvests of a fruitful life are in the intangible yield of presenting your spouse holy before God, of having children of godly character, and of seeing your own character shaped to resemble His more closely. As you rearrange your life to accommodate home-based work, be sure that you are not so overwhelmed with the activity of the day that you neglect what is fruitful.

Home-work intensifies the tension between activity and fruitfulness. When you're working at home, you're operating in a compressed feedback loop. The link between your work and the fruit of it is much shorter.

In a traditional job, the payback loop is elongated. Spending some overtime on a project brings it in on time and achieves the team's goal, resulting a few months later in a good review and a raise. The route that your work takes to eventually benefit your family is a circuitous one. When you work at home, the reason why you're working and the impact of your work commitments and schedule are much more immediately apparent.

When I work overtime, I'm directly taking time away from my husband and children. I'm not away in an office building miles away, out of sight and out of mind. I'm quite specifically not in the kitchen, not playing Monopoly, or not gardening in the backyard. On the other hand, when I get the extra-generous check from that overtime work, I can show my patient family the direct result of that effort.

The intimacy of home-work can also be a powerful motivator.

Your family isn't "out there" at school, in day care or wherever. They are right there. Seeing, again, your son in jeans he's rapidly outgrowing can be just the impetus to make another sales call.

Rest Time, Not Overtime

How can you keep this sense of immediacy from eroding into pressure?

First and foremost, pray for your career. Pray generally, that God will give you wisdom and guidance so that you will not feel that you are shouldering the burdens alone. Pray blessings on your clients, customers, and employer. Whether they know it or not, they are part of God's good will for you and part of His plan for your well-being.

I pray that my clients will enjoy harmonious relationships in their work places. I also pray that they'll make wise business decisions and will be profitable. I pray that I'll be a valuable asset to them, understanding their needs and easy to work with.

Pray that your children will have a heart-level grasp of why your decision to work from home is motivated by love for them. Seek opportunities to explicitly exhibit to them biblical behavior and character—honesty, wisdom, respect for others, prudence. (If you start to run out of specific ideas, try praying through some of the Proverbs. I guarantee that your focus will be restored.)

Another way to fertilize your field, so to speak, is to honor the Sabbath. As my husband likes to say, "God needed a break. So do I!" Giving in to the temptation to sneak in a little work on Sunday can be insidious. The first time, you just review your plans for the coming week. The second time, you write a few letters or generate a few invoices. All of a sudden, you're counting on that time and you've just become a victim of fruitless activity. God is the one who made the week with six work days and one rest day. Give in to the reality of it and enjoy it.

A corollary to the Sunday sabbath is the idea of a personal sabbath time. Some people call this "feeding your soul." It is hard to overemphasize the importance of reserving some aspect of life that is pure enjoyment.

At about the same time that I started the travel newsletter, which took about thirty hours a week on top of my other commitments, I confounded and amused my friends by joining a sewing group called the Smart Smockers. It is an artisan guild that concentrates on the relatively obscure needlecrafts of smocking (which is embroidery over pleated fabric), antique-reproduction sewing techniques, and other time-consuming fancywork.

Going to Smart Smocker meetings is one of the highlights of my month. Members bring in projects (they're supposed to be completed), and we all admire each other's creations. We eat cookies and spend hours discussing arcane minutia of the craft. It's a delightful change of pace.

Feeling Burned Out?

If you don't already know what feeds your soul, find out. It's all too easy for business and family responsibilities to soak up all your time. Whatever it is that is precious to you, make it a top priority. Enjoy it without reservation or apology.

There are consequences of not doing so. You'll not only be frustrated because you never find time for yourself, but you'll also be courting burnout.

Some signs of impending burnout are:
- you're no longer enjoying your devotional or family life
- you feel like you're always playing catch-up
- instead of running your life, it's running you and you feel like you're about to be run over
- your patience is worn thin, especially with your family
- you have a sense of overall weariness
- you are struggling with frustration, feelings of failure, and guilt—and you feel like they're winning
- you rarely get time off
- you're not exercising as you should
- serving God with gladness is no longer a primary characteristic of your life—you feel like running away from God and your life
- life feels like a trap

If this sounds all too familiar, stop and let Jesus restore you. Reaffirm Him as Lord of your life and lover of your soul through worship and confession. Listen to some of your favorite Christian music. Some people find it helpful to spend a night or longer in solitude at a retreat house. Or, have a home retreat and get everyone else to leave. (Ask nicely.)

When you recognize some of these symptoms cropping up, try to head them off with a quick picker-upper. I like to have lunch and shop with my twelve year old (as long as she's not comparison shopping for some mythical perfect outfit). Have lunch with an old friend who means it when she asks you how you're doing. Take a romantic getaway weekend with your husband. Eat chocolate.

Don't forget to examine the circumstances that pushed you to the edge. Figure out what needs to change so that you avoid a repeat performance.

Self-Discipline, Not Self-Flagellation

As far as I can tell, there are two characteristics that you absolutely must cultivate to successfully work from home. You must be a self-starter. And you must be a self-stopper.

Most work-from-home experts carry on endlessly about the importance of self-discipline. To a person, they are referring to the need to get up on time in the morning, stick with a job till it's done to the client's satisfaction, and stay on top of paperwork, especially tax and financial filings.

If you struggle with this, you need to figure out why you cannot get going and carry through. Perhaps you aren't motivated; maybe your goals and objectives don't move you to action. If that is the case, you'd better revamp your goals and/or objectives.

Some people have never developed good work habits. They are the college classmates who fluffed off all semester and then pulled all-nighters to get their term papers done (and drove the rest of us crazy by getting A's). You may be able to get through college and even grad school that way, but sloppy work habits will handicap you over the long haul.

Consider asking someone to hold you accountable for how you use your time. Get a good personal organizing system like Day Runner or Filofax and develop the habit of using it faithfully. If self-starting difficulties seem to be simply a byproduct of switching to the unstructured home-work day, recall times when you were self-disciplined. See what factors or circumstances you can recreate in your home business to help you get some momentum. For instance, if you previously found it helpful to end each day reviewing the next day's appointments and to-do list, revive that habit. Maybe writing up your day's goals on a self-stick note and putting it on the bathroom mirror will be enough to jog you into action.

Rarely examined is the importance of knowing when to quit. I don't mean giving up entirely, though it's certainly important to discern when it's time to shut down an unprofitable and fruitless enterprise. Rather, I am referring to the everyday discipline of physically and mentally leaving the office. Some people cope with this by artificially setting hours that they stick with as though they were working in a corporation. They rarely make exceptions, even if it means inconveniencing themselves by, say, grocery shopping at the height of the rush hour crush.

The more you settle in to your home-work situation, the less likely you are to stick to a rigid schedule. You'll probably find yourself tossing some laundry into the washer when you're waiting for clients to return a phone call. You may write a letter to your grandmother as a break from processing orders. It will feel natural to invite one of your children's friends (well-behaved, of course) over to play while you're finishing up a project on the computer.

At times, the pressure to keep at it day and night can be rooted in a deeper place. If your family is sacrificing and scrimping to free up cash for your business venture, you may feel that you have to work straight through until you've recouped the investment. Even if you know that you're operating way beyond the point of diminishing returns—working harder and harder for less and less—it still may feel impossible to slow down and take regular breaks. If the pressure is aggravated by overwhelming household needs, consider getting some type of household help.

A Potential Collision Course

Another source of tension can be attempting to mix ministry and money. Hire people who are qualified for the job and who you think will be good employees. You will have to decide for yourself if you want to make active Christian faith a prerequisite for anyone working for you. However, beware of taking someone on simply because you feel sorry for them or because you feel obliged to hire a Christian. If you do, you may end up in a very sticky situation where your employer-employee relationship is muddied by varying interpretations of how the Bible says we are to handle disputes among believers and so on.

Again, go back to your goals. If your ministry objective is to help the poor, and you see job training as part of that, separate that from your business goals. Focus on ministry through church and parachurch channels to keep it cleanly separate from your business.

Don't Overload Your Circuits

Most of us can only tolerate so much upheaval at once. Exercise common sense when you're thinking about establishing home-work. If you're moving, one of your parents has just died, and your child was just diagnosed with asthma, put it off for a while. A period of extreme emotional stress would also preclude an immediate change. It's more prudent to make a strong start a little later than to alienate clients and customers by starting and stalling and starting again.

Another consideration is the ages, developmental stages, and personalities of your children. How many you have and plan to add is important, too. If you have several preschoolers, it's probably not wise to launch a jewelry-making business and work with open trays of beads, charms, and wire from the dining room table. You will find yourself vacuuming up your raw materials. Working from home may give you more resources to deal with young or difficult children, but it will not give you infinite resources.

If you are established in a traditional job, and your desire to move home is a reaction to circumstances there with which you're unhappy, proceed carefully. It may be that other options will be more beneficial to you and your family. Consider all the factors that are feeding the unacceptable situation and see how they also will be affected if you are working from home.

At Home or from Home

Home-based business is just that—based at home. Some jobs are performed almost completely at home. Mail-order, telecommuting, and desktop publishing are like that. Workers leave only for errands and sales calls. With other careers, there's a certain amount of paperwork that's done at home, but the actual job is done out of the house. For instance, preparation for corporate training seminars can be done at home, but the actual seminars are held at the client's site.

Many positions let the balance of at-home and from-home-work vary from client to client, seasonally, or according to your personal and family preference. Consulting, project-oriented work, and crafts manufacture, among others, offer maximum flexibility.

Many people open home businesses because they want to exert

greater control over their lives. Certainly, working from home affords greater flexibility. It's important to recognize, though, that there will still be many things that you can't control. You will still suffer from miscommunications, lost orders, and crabby customers or overbearing clients. Thinking that you will be your own boss is a fallacy. You will be trading a single boss for multiple bosses, because each customer you serve is, in effect, a boss; so is each client.

In a corporate environment, the only people who deal directly with customers are sales and customer service reps. Their demands are filtered through the layers of bureaucracy and interpreted many times before they reach the typical employee. When you are on your own, that buffer is gone. For better or worse, you will be getting direct feedback from your customers and clients. When they are happy with what you've done for them, this will be a pleasant experience. When they're not, it can evoke discouragement, frustration, defensiveness, and anger.

Some types of home-based work also afford the chance to determine your own hours. You can design your own flextime, working ten hours a day, three days a week. If you work best during the early morning, you can schedule a 7:00 A.M. to noon workday. The main constraint you'll have is working around clients and customers stuck in the nine to five workday. Even if it's inconvenient for you, you'll have to accommodate their hours in your day.

Michelene is the mother of preschool twins and a baby. Before she had her children, she worked as a buyer for a Christian card and gift shop, and then as a gift and housewares buyer for a hardware store. She wants to keep her selling skills somewhat intact, but isn't interested in a full-scale career while her children are very young. Her solution has been to become a Tupperware representative. She clusters the demonstration parties at times of peak demand and then goes for weeks without organizing one. Though she's a popular rep and gets many repeat bookings, she is pacing herself for the long term. Her earnings are only about one thousand dollars a year, but she is achieving her goal—keeping her sales abilities fresh and gradually building experience with the company.

When you keep your assignments from God clear, you won't be taking on what's not from Him. Keeping your load in line may involve decisions as trivial as signing up to help with a PTA fundraiser twice a year instead of monthly. Or you may have more difficult situations, like dropping a client who is always calling at the last minute and demanding extra service that clashes with family time. Set your priorities and let God take care of the fallout.

The Marketing Mentality

In the prior chapter, we touched on the importance of understanding that self-employed and alternative career trackworkers are always selling their ability and track records.

Developing and maintaining a marketing mentality is not as burdensome as it sounds. Keep in mind that marketing is understanding and anticipating your clients', customers', and employers' needs. You will probably employ a variety of means to let your potential clients and customers know of your services and products. Sales is moving to specifically address those needs in a way that benefits both you and them.

Presumably, you're pursuing a business or career that's interesting to you, so you aren't trying to whip up a false level of enthusiasm. It shouldn't feel burdensome to stay abreast of general economic and business news and trends so that you can pick up on issues that are likely to affect your clientele.

Marketing support materials like your logo, brochures, product information, catalog, and packaging will all communicate your business's image. Writing articles that appear in trade or professional journals is a major way to bolster credibility. Public relations efforts, such as sending well-written and timely press releases to trade and general interest publications; cooperating with major customers and clients on their public relations campaigns; and giving away products or services to local charities to auction will gradually build your reputation in the community and with your target market. You may give free informational seminars or do guest speaking to colleges, professional groups, chambers of commerce, and other audiences with an interest in your specialty.

Marketing encompasses ongoing research, sales, follow-up, service, and continual communication to resell to the same audience. Advertising, on the other hand, is specifically geared to make a sales pitch to a defined group of current or potential customers or clients.

Sooner or later you'll be asked to give away your product or service. Then you'll have to tiptoe your way over a slippery path, trying to keep your goodwill and reputation intact while not giving away the store. I gladly donate copies of my books to local silent auctions and other fundraisers (at least, to support causes I agree with). That's good public relations.

I also get calls from acquaintances and even other writers who are seeking information about Midwest family travel. At that point, I have to find out what I'm going to get back in exchange for the information, which is, of course, what my readers pay for. If I think I'll get some publicity from the request, I comply. But if someone hasn't bought the newsletter or book and isn't a member of the media, I direct them to my publications. Why give away my prime asset?

If you are telecommuting or working a flexible career path at a corporation, your ongoing marketing will take a different form. It's still crucial to stay informed about what's going in your field, your company's industry, and with the economy in general. Use this information to stay in the communications loop at work. When you're able to demonstrate on an ongoing basis that you're still looking out for the interests of the company, you're underscoring that you're still part of the team.

We'll take a closer look at developing and maintaining a solid relationship with your employer in chapter seven. For now, suffice it to say now that it's imperative to always be looking at how your alternative career track is benefiting your employer.

Employee Relations

Sooner or later, you will probably have to deal with the mushrooming trend of independent contractors. In the past, independent contractors have been self-employed people who had a variety of clients. Recently, though, it has become a euphemism for essentially hiring someone full time but yet not granting them the benefits of being an employee. Some corporations have staged mass layoffs and have then quietly hired back some workers as so-called independent contractors. Under the guise of giving the former employees the chance to be self-employed with all the flexible advantages that entails, the employer assigns virtually the same work load and responsibilities, minus the job security and expectation of raises, and with no fringe benefits.

Accepting a modified independent contractor position may fit your needs if it does allow genuine self-direction. You may welcome the drawbacks if flexibility is of paramount importance to you. However, be sure that the set-up does not slide into exploitation. As this was being written, the IRS was investigating possibly fraudulent arrangements to determine if many independent contractors were in fact employees. (If so, the employer would be liable legally for tax collection and related paperwork, and ethically for a host of other related benefits and issues.)

Don't let yourself be cheated out of the benefits that are due legitimate employees. Just because you are working from home does not make you an independent contractor. It gets even muddier when you consider that many home-work situations could be constructed in any of several ways. For instance, if you handle an annual, major market research project for your employer, you could break out that project alone as a part-time job and do it in the office with flexible hours; you could conduct the research from home and telecommute, yet still remain an employee; or you could become a bona fide consultant and handle that project, along with other research projects, from your home office.

Giving the Worker His or Her Due

This touchy issue can also come up when you are the employer. It's tempting to label your workers independent contractors to avoid the myriad hassles of complying with tax, worker's compensation, and other paperwork. As well, they are then responsible for their own overhead, phone, transportation, and other costs of doing business. They submit to you one bill for their services and expenses and do their own filings and accounting. If you subcontract with people who are truly self-employed, you should have no problems. However, you are asking for trouble if you pretend that your employees are really self-employed.

You will run into this issue again when you hire household help. Even a monthly cleaning lady counts as an employee, according to IRS regulations. Domestics who come to your house weekly or daily are almost certain to qualify. Complicating this scenario is the fact that many domestic workers prefer to get under-the-table cash wages because they don't want to subtract taxes from their earnings.

How can you tell the difference between someone who is truly self-employed and an independent contractor who is really not? According to Paladin, a human resource consulting firm, and the

Bureau of National Affairs, a national research and publishing firm, these are a few qualifications of employees:

- the employer has the right to "direct and control" the worker's methods and details of the work
- the employer supplies training to the worker
- the employer insists on specifying who does the work
- the employer relies on the worker exclusively to perform work at frequently recurring intervals, even when the work is part-time.

The BNA also recommends considering whether or not the supposed independent contractor can work for another company at any time. True independents can, with no conflict of interest issues; employees cannot. Incorporating yourself or your business (as opposed to remaining a proprietorship or partnership) will go a long way toward protecting independent contractor status.

For more details on determining the legal status of independent contractors, see the resource list in chapter ten.

Margaret's Story, Part Two

Independent contractor status is one of several issues that Margaret, whom you met in chapter three, is thinking about as she continues to sort out her imminent reentry into the job market.

Because Darch's benefit package is sufficient for their needs, she's not under pressure to find a position that delivers medical and dental coverage and other fringe benefits. That gives her the freedom to consider the whole spectrum of flexible and home-work opportunities.

Margaret eliminated the painted-sneaker idea. Though it would have been fun, she doubted that she would make a decent hourly wage. As well, the relentless round of weekend craft fairs, where such items are typically sold, would force her to jettison her work with children's church.

It's possible that Margaret could eventually get work in illustration or creating Sunday school curriculum, but she knew it would take a long time to build a client base in both areas.

Considering the immediate need for income, she turned her attention instead to keyline and paste-up, the skill that is most likely to result in work right away. Her medium-term goal is to set up stable relationships with two to four corporate clients.

She called several dozen advertising agencies and print shops and found about eight that hire free-lancers. Now she's setting up interviews with them to show her portfolio and inquire about their specific needs. She has already completed one interview and was told she'd be considered for free-lance work as it becomes available.

While she's pursuing work, she is continuing to research the market. Margaret is getting together with graphic artists both free-lance and corporate to find out what graphics and desktop publishing software is most commonly used, what hourly rates are customary, and what magazines and professional groups she should become familiar with.

Margaret has also taken steps to address her self-diagnosed difficulty with self-discipline. "I can stay active all day long but I don't necessarily get to the big things, my priorities," she says.

She has asked a very organized and disciplined woman leader in her church to meet with her and hold her accountable for moving forward on her career aspirations. "Having someone else know that I failed to do something I'd said I'd do is embarrassing enough to motivate me," she says. "Once you get the work, you have to meet the deadline, so there's a structure imposed on you."

Margaret and Darch are going to track her income and related expenses as the work starts to come in. If her after-tax income isn't enough to help out with the home improvement costs, plus pay for software training and other investments in Margaret's career, they'll consider other options. One is to find a part-time job that would be less challenging creatively but would minimize child care costs and complications. Another choice is for Margaret to take a full-time position where she can become adept at using state-of-the-art computer graphics software. If she does take a full-time job, Margaret hopes that she may be able to negotiate flextime or an alternative career track after a couple of years.

Don't Be Blinded by Ambition

To date, Margaret has been content with her decisions. She hasn't regretted staying home with Matthew and investing in spiritual and personal growth.

It's all too easy to lose sight of these greater things in the crush of daily deadlines, meetings, and job-related frictions. All too often, these pressures can push a healthy desire to be productive into an unhealthy ambition. You don't have to be working eighty hours a week in a fiftieth-floor office to be consumed by the desire to do a bit more, a bit better, and certainly to best the next person. That's when the ambition that gives you a creative edge starts cutting you.

Curb out-of-bounds ambition with contentment. When you're getting the message from clients, your boss, and your checkbook that the only way to get ahead is to work harder, smarter, and longer, retreat to the truths that have held through the ages.

Take a spiritual inventory of the times that God has provided even when your faith was at low tide. Call to mind those moments when He has felt as close as a breeze on your cheek. Extend your hands to Him, open to receive peace. Savor the blessings that already enrich your life. Pray for the mind of the Lord which shakes the wheat from the chaff and sorts the jewels from the stones. Cultivate thankfulness, especially in a bounty of opportunities!

· 5 ·

Starting a Business

THE VAST MAJORITY of American consumers don't know what heirloom sewing is. If they did know, they probably wouldn't care.

Not only does Linda know, but she has built a half-million dollar home-based mail-order business in this very small niche market.

For years Linda worked as an intensive care nurse. For relaxation, she indulged in heirloom sewing—smocking dresses for her young daughter Dana and making Victorian-style blouses from fine imported fabrics and laces for herself.

The satisfactions of nursing, though, began to fade for Linda. She wanted a flexible schedule that would adapt to her husband's travel obligations, and she wanted to be on hand to help at Dana's Christian elementary school. A home-based business seemed to fit the bill.

One day in 1987, she was telling her husband how frustrated she was with the hassles of ordering all her specialty sewing supplies by mail from dozens of small companies.

"There was nobody who offered everything," she recalls. "And I thought, 'I wish there was somebody out there who offered free shipping and handling.' And David said, 'Well, why don't you try it?' "

It took fifteen thousand dollars to buy inventory, pay for initial advertising, print a catalog, and finance other sundry start-up costs. The first few months were nail–biters. But the company was profitable in its first year, and sales have doubled every year since. Linda estimates that 1993 gross sales will top five hundred thousand dollars. Now that her company is one of the dominant forces in its estimated $3 million market, its rate of growth will probably slow somewhat.

That's all right with Linda, who could use a breather.

She now has seven part-time employees who work with her on an as-needed basis, keeping her data base updated, filling orders, and restocking. (Dana, now ten, earns two dollars per hour packaging orders and writing thank-you notes.)

The company operates from the barely finished basement of Linda's suburban Colonial-style house. Homemade shelves hold bolts of fabrics. Boxes of patterns and stacks of books are neatly piled on tables. With two phone lines, Linda takes orders at her old, scratched wooden desk or at her kitchen counter when she's making dinner.

"All the compartments of my life have fuzzy edges. I feel that I have a really integrated approach to work. When I'm cooking, I'll be answering calls and jotting things down," she says. "I think the buzzword is 'multitasking,' which is funny because women have been doing it for five thousand years. Women are used to doing ten things at once."

Still, she can't do everything. "Working at home, you see all the things that you'd like to do for your family—baking bread or cookies—when before you didn't even see the possibilities," she says ruefully. "Having a focus [on the business] means that there are some things you aren't looking at."

Best of all, she's making more money than she did as a nurse. To earn that money she works at least sixty-five hours a week. So far, she hasn't taken more than five consecutive days away from the company. Her main sources of relaxation are following her favorite baseball team and two weekly meetings—one a Bible study and the other with a prayer partner.

Now that Linda has assembled a team of employees trained in various tasks, she is enjoying some relaxation from the constant pressure of running the company.

So far, she has resolved the issue of whether to seek out Christians exclusively to work for her by trusting God to direct her to the right employees. "I put an ad in the paper for an administrative assistant, but I didn't know how to word it. You can't just say, 'If you feel God leading you, call,' or, 'Prayerfully consider this position.'

"Forty-five people responded. I felt the Lord directing me to this one person, so I called her. She said, 'You know, I was just praying, "Lord, if you want me to have this position, just open the door." ' She wanted to be able to work her schedule around one day a week at the local crisis pregnancy center."

With such obvious leading as that, Linda immediately hired her. Her assistant spends twenty-four to thirty hours a week on paperwork at Linda's as well as her time at the center.

Not coincidentally, a few weeks after the assistant came on board, she and Linda ended up in an involved conversation with a regular customer whose husband was pressuring her to have an abortion. At forty-one, the woman was apprehensive about the chances of having a baby with birth defects. She was "tied up in knots," she said, about having diagnostic tests performed.

"We just gently told her, 'Hey, you'll have to live with the consequences of this,' " relates Linda. "I told her to follow God's leading in her heart. Last I'd heard, she'd decided to just let nature take its course and have the baby. We still pray for her. Our customers now will call us if they have a big prayer need.

"We try to bring the Lord into what we do—we say 'God Bless You' on some of our sales newsletters," says Linda. "I think that the Lord has enabled me to hear those little nuances that let me know that people need a friend that day, and I can pray for them over the phone. It's my business. I can do it if I want."

Linda has found that she has more control over her work environment and her emotional reactions to work than she did previously. "It's so much less pressure than nursing. If I really screw up an order, I can do what is needed to make it up to the customer," she says.

Working from home has provided Linda the opportunity to spend more focused time with David and to volunteer at Dana's school. She also extends personal flexibility to her employees, who are expected to work around their children's schedules and can bring babies to work with them.

Linda feels that running the company provides more satisfaction than nursing. As a nurse, she never felt as though her work was completed. Now she has a sense of finality when certain segments of the job—getting out her monthly sales newsletter, for example—are finally finished.

"This is a safeguard for my family. It is truly a family business," Linda says.

Meet the Boss—Look in the Mirror!

Starting your own business is scary and exciting. This is the most flexible home-work option and, some would say, the one with the greatest potential benefits. However, it's also the most demanding option, both financially and emotionally. According to Dun & Bradstreet's report on business failures, over 50 percent of new businesses fail within five years.

It's also the option that's most difficult to "shut the door on" when the workday is supposed to be done. Business owners cannot have a half-hearted attitude about their venture. In order to make it work, they live, breathe, eat, and sleep their business.

In some ways, you are your own boss—but you probably never worked for anyone so demanding. Especially in the beginning, before you can afford help, you do everything from visiting the banker to making the photocopies. It's easy to get worn down and lose sight of why you got into this thing to begin with. Further, if you carry the "I'm the boss" attitude to its extreme, you'll structure your business for your own convenience and to suit your own needs, not those of your customers—a situation that will inevitably prove self-defeating.

Think before You Jump

Successful entrepreneurs report that they are constantly being asked by people how they came up with their business concept.

Few people sit bolt upright in bed in the middle of the night with a blockbuster idea. Virtually everyone starts by researching business angles of services, ideas, or products that they are already interested in.

Greg Harris, founder of the Home & Family Business Workshop, which operates seminars on starting and growing home-based businesses, says that he encourages erstwhile entrepreneurs to begin with considering this question: What do you love to do, without regard for profits?

"People shouldn't look for where the money is. They should look ahead to where they'd like to be when they're successful. Don't pick a business until you've picked a field," he advises.

Then the long process of research begins. Attending trade shows, reading trade magazines, talking to people in all kinds of businesses in the field, and "trying on" various ideas that occur to you are aspects of the initial stage. Expect to spend up to nine months diligently researching before you feel you have a thorough overview of the concept.

"Once you get into the field, you'll discover all kinds of niche opportunities you can take advantage of," says Greg. He relates the story of one man who loved dogs and thought he might like to go into dog breeding. However, his research yielded the discouraging information that there are hundreds of dog breeders already competing with each other. As he continued his inquiries, he found that there was a need for people to organize and promote dog shows. He's now happily doing just that.

"Expect your ultimate bread-and-butter service to be a distant relative of what you're actually starting," says Greg. "Take a stepping-stone approach to business ventures."

Finding the right niche is not always a straight-line journey. Jim spent six years running a greeting card company. That paved the way for his current venture, a small publishing company. And because of his publishing experience, he recently started organizing university book fairs.

"Home business income is not always steady," he says. "It ebbs and flows. Sometimes it ebbs more than it flows."

Jim's latest product is a small business how-to magazine that's distributed on computer disc through the shareware network. (Shareware is software that's distributed for free; users buy it only after they've tried it.) He advertises it via on-line computer networks and through shareware catalogs.

Find the Customers First

Develop your marketing strategy in tandem with your business concept. As you come to know the market, you'll also get to know how customers find out about products and services in the category and how they go about buying them.

Mail order and direct selling (like party-plan sales organizations) usually invite close contact with customers. When you can have an ongoing dialogue with your customers, it's easier to detect demand for new products and shift your operations to accommodate customers' needs. However, Greg cautions, taking a premature and scattershot approach to mail order can soak up precious seed money with little return.

"You can get started in it if you have a close association with the people you're trying to sell to. But if you're just renting mailing lists, you'll just break even until you have your own house list," he predicts.

Consider Ruth and Jerry's strategy. They are the couple who started the mail-order catalog for CD storage units. Their ultimate goal is to grow a home business with enough profit to support them, but they are not expecting that to happen overnight. They're taking cautious, carefully considered steps and expecting that it will take at least three years before they start to make a significant amount of money.

The catalog is an outgrowth of Jerry's longtime hobby of collecting and wholesaling vintage records. Through his "paying hobby," as it were, he was already familiar with the stereo aficionado market.

The idea of launching a catalog devoted to CD storage equipment and related accessories occurred to him in mid-1990. By June 1991, he had collected the necessary paperwork—toll-free phone number, required tax forms, supplier relationships—and started advertising.

As we've already learned, God responded generously to the family's prayers for orders. In its first year of operation, the catalog operation lost $1,000. In 1992, it had a gross income of $1,250; in the first six weeks of 1993, gross revenues were $7,500. Ruth projects that it will turn a profit of $3,000 to $4,000 by year's-end. She is evaluating the profits, expenses, and efforts at each new level of sales.

At this point, she is spending about fifteen hours a week on the operation, taking and filling orders and working on the paperwork. "I don't have the fear that if I don't cut corners here and there and cheat people I won't make money. It's all up to God," she says. "I deal fairly and honestly with people; it's my best chance of letting God do what He wants to with the business. In the long run, we'll have to decide if it's worth the money we're making."

Be a Link in a Chain

Home-based franchises are one of the fastest-growing small business categories today. They combine some of the advantages of working from home (low overhead, flexible hours) with some of the advantages of joining up with a big corporation (sophisticated marketing, management advice). A well-run franchise will be able to present proof of the its track record.

However, buying into a franchise plunges you into the business, allowing for little time to get your feet wet gradually. Franchise fees and related start-up costs vary widely, from as little as two thousand dollars to thirty thousand dollars and more. As well, part of the franchise agreement will stipulate the percentage of gross revenues that you will be obliged to send to headquarters. As a franchise owner, you'll have some input into corporate policy, but there will be times when you may have to make the best of their decisions. But there's no doubt that these packaged concepts are ready-made for entrepreneurs who are eager to get started.

When Diane discovered Computertots, she knew that it was the fit she'd been looking for. She had experience as director of a day-care center and she had done office support work for the owner of another home-based franchise. In every job she'd had, she had most enjoyed two things: administration and working with children. Her day-care position had allowed her to be with her two sons during the day, but once they started school, she wanted to be at home when they left and came back. She was researching home-based franchises in 1990 when she learned about Computertots.

"What they did matched what I wanted to do," she says. As soon as the franchise for her portion of a major metropolitan area became available, she bought it. Typical set-up costs for a Computertots operator include a $19,500 franchise fee plus an additional $6,000 for equipment, insurance, and working capital. The royalty fee is 6 percent of gross receipts.

Diane spends much of her fifty hours a week of work time selling the Computertots concept to day-care and preschool teachers. The franchise teachers bring a portable computer to the center or school and operate introductory computer courses for children whose parents have signed them up. Tuition runs up to thirty-four dollars per child for a month's worth of half-hour classes.

It's a no-hassle way for the center or school to broaden their curriculum, and parents welcome the chance to give their child a specialized enrichment class during regular school hours, instead of using up precious weekend time. The franchise signs up parents directly and handles all the billing and marketing.

Diane employs twenty teachers, each of whom works up to fifteen hours a week. She had no background in computer education when she started, and doesn't expect her teachers to be adept at computers, either. "I tell them, 'If we're going to teach a three-year-old to use the computer, I hope we can teach you!' " she says.

While she counts her relationships with her teachers as one of the best parts of the job, she has also learned to set firm limits to protect her family time. Her Computertots phone is set up to ring only in her home office. "That way, if I'm not in my office, I don't pick up the phone," she explains. She checks messages hourly until 9:00 P.M., then she calls it quits. Teachers know that it's only permissible to contact her on her car phone in the case of a dire emergency, such as a complete failure of one of the computers half an hour before a class is to start.

Diane is making more money than she had at either of her previous jobs—enough that her husband has been freed to leave his position with a major law firm and join a small firm close to the couple's home, enabling him to spend more time with his sons.

The Real Bottom Line

Counting the cost is essential before throwing open the doors of a new business. You'll need to consider financial investment as well as the pressures the company will bring to your family. After all, it's in their home too.

Building a business takes more than an interest in the field and technical expertise in one specific area of operations. Don't overestimate your management skills. Unless you've run a company before, you probably are accustomed to seeing only one portion of overall operations. Evaluate your experience in sales, planning, operations, financial management; be quick to admit what you don't know and seek expert help.

Check and double-check your market research. Be sure that a demand for your product or service exists before you sink big bucks into the idea. Simply identifying an unfilled market niche does not mean that a profitable opportunity exists. There may be very good reasons why the niche is empty, i.e., others have tried to fill it and have failed. If the unfilled market need is glaringly obvious, it's likely that others have considered it and rejected it. Do some research to find out if that's so, and why. Try to learn from others' mistakes.

Entrepreneurs perennially underestimate the amount of money it will require to carry their concept to fruition. "Regardless of your financial situation, pretend you are poor and get into business at the lowest possible threshold," says Greg. "This is not very encouraging for people who want to make money fast."

He also warns against the false assumption that just because you're making a certain amount of money operating a small business part time, profits will increase in proportion to the additional time you devote to it. "Start something and get it going before you count on it to take care of you," he says. One commonly accepted rule of thumb is to take your best estimate of how long it will take to turn a profit—and double it.

"It costs so much money to grow the company that you don't see coming back to you right away," Linda laments. "I send out catalogs, and many people don't order for six months. When you're sending out five hundred of them, it really adds up. Those are periods of high growth when you're investing in the future."

If spending more time with your family is one of your objectives, scale back your plans. It's much easier to expand a business that is making money with only twenty-five hours a week worth of work than it is to try to salvage the successful segments of one that's losing money overall, and takes sixty-five hours a week.

As you're putting in your long hours, spend some mental energy thinking through how you'll use employees when you can finally afford them. Would you prefer to be pushed up from below, as it were, to a management spot, by delegating important tasks like new product development, advertising, or sales? Or would you rather keep your favorite part of the job and have lots of administrative help? If you're a team player who's going it alone, the solution may be to bring in a partner whose experience and strengths complement yours.

Don't Zone Out

A related issue is just where you'll put your employees. Local zoning ordinances will probably prohibit you from having more than two or three employees at the house who aren't family members. Other typical restrictions prohibit using a garage or backyard structure as a warehouse. It's imperative to check with municipal authorities to be sure you're complying with zoning and home-business ordinances. Condominium and subdivision homeowners' associations may have restrictions on home businesses as well.

Most complaints about home businesses are lodged by neighbors. Usually they are upset that traffic to and from the business is complicating their access to the street and parking. One neighbor filed a complaint against the home workers next door because the UPS truck habitually parked in her driveway to deliver and pick up packages to the business.

Adopting a proactive stance is a good way to head off conflict with neighbors. Offer to take in their packages when they're at work or on vacation. Maybe volunteering to head up a neighborhood watch group will position your at-home status as a neighborhood asset. Then you'll have a bank of goodwill to draw on when you do host a meeting of six people and they park on the street for a couple hours. Complying with municipal ordinances can force you to come up with some creative alternatives.

Another way to manage expansion is to keep your office at home but shift the bulk of your operations elsewhere. Some mail-order operations arrange with major suppliers to have merchandise drop-shipped directly from the manufacturer, though it's being billed to the purchaser by the mail-order firm. Consider renting commercial space for your operation, particularly if you find yourself awash in raw materials, inventory, and shipping supplies.

The most important part of an entrepreneurial venture is your family's support. If they want to help out, involve them as much as you can. Even small children can contribute by helping to clean the office (especially if it's their toys littering the floor!). I sometimes hire my daughters to do simple filing. They know the alphabet better than I do, anyway. When everyone is invested in the effort, the profit-sharing is all the richer.

❖6❖

Consulting and Free-lancing

ONE MONDAY MORNING, a client called Nancy at about 8:30. "Did you try to fax us something over the weekend?" she inquired. "There's something here that looks like a Teenage Mutant Ninja Turtle sewing pattern envelope, size small. It has your fax identification number on it."

Moments like this do happen. It's bad enough when we experience collision between our roles as parents and home workers, but it's worse when our kids start initiating close encounters with the clients.

With three children ages six and under, role collision is something that Nancy is more than familiar with. Since 1987, she has operated a specialized accounting service full time from her home office.

Both Nancy and her clients maintain an air of amused tolerance towards the playfulness of her children. "Once they were too quiet. When I checked, they were painting their finger- and toenails with white-out," Nancy laughs. "They're supposed to stay on their side of the basement (it's divided into playroom and office), and sometimes I put a gate up. But the older ones have figured out how to crawl under the desks."

After she graduated from a prestigious university, Nancy took a "low-level clerical job" with a small financial planning firm. A series of jolting changes at the firm, including the death of the owner, forced her to rapidly learn the intricacies of accounting for the firm's primary client base, commercial singers and small advertising agencies. Later in the same year, her husband developed the first in what would prove to be a series of eye problems. His sight is expected to deteriorate to the point of legal blindness within a decade.

"Until then, I was waiting around to be a full-time mom," Nancy says. "Then I started thinking, maybe it would be good for me to have some kind of part-time work."

The firm changed hands, and Nancy and the new owner clashed. At that point, she realized that knowing the ins and outs of the complicated clerical and accounting work was advantageous. "I knew the mechanics of the business and I was cross-trained in the other functions," she explains. "I had clients approaching me to go on my own. I knew I could do it, and I thought, What do I have to lose? Clients will either come to me or they won't."

Nancy and her husband took out a five thousand dollar bank loan, which they could easily pay back on just his income. She bought the necessary equipment—office furniture, computer, phones, and fax—and set up shop in her basement.

Thanks to her excellent reputation (and also to her employer's abrasive personality), several clients immediately moved their accounts to Nancy's fledgling business. "Because this is my little niche, I'm also able to give them good advice on other aspects of their operations that helps make their financial structure more efficient and profitable," Nancy points out. "In our highly specialized society you need a lot of experts. And that's what I am."

When she started, Nancy recalls, "I thought, 'If I can squeak five years out of this, I'll be satisfied.' " Shortly thereafter, she had her first child and expanded her client base. Her husband's condition worsened.

"A few year ago, I was looking to some point in the future when I would retire," she says with only a trace of regret. "I don't think that way anymore. My work is really a gift from God. There's a sense that this road was paved and I just walked on it."

These days, Nancy is in her basement office working over forty hours a week. Her children spend about thirty-five hours a week with a neighborhood woman who operates a home day-care center. Sitting at her desk, Nancy can look past her computer screen and see a chalkboard easel, a child-sized table and chairs, and a huge toy chest overflowing with dolls and Ninja turtles. Her children frequently play in her office in the evening while Nancy finishes up projects in half-hour snatches.

"I've spent many times with a child on my lap on a pillow nursing while I'm talking on the phone," she says. "I'm just glad my clients can't see me.

"There's a sense that God is ordering my days. On Thursdays, when I have the kids most of the day, it's usually quiet. It's like God knows I can't answer twenty calls. He holds them off until Friday morning."

Nancy wishes she could find a partner who shares her penchant for perfectionism—one of the traits that has endeared her to her clients. So far, the right match hasn't emerged, though it's not for lack of trying.

The flexibility of her situation was underscored when her third child was born with birth defects requiring hospitalization and surgery. Despite the seemingly endless round of doctor's appointments, Nancy was able to keep a basic momentum going at work.

It has been a lucrative niche for her. She earns fully half of the family's income. Her current goal is to pay off the mortgage within five years so that the family can thrive on a reduced income when her husband's sight deteriorates to the point where it hampers his ability to work.

Her major expenses are domestic: $450 a week for child care, preschool tuition, and a twice-a-month cleaning lady. "I think I have the best person for my kids, and she's entitled to a living wage," Nancy says. "It's also a function of God blessing me. How could I not bless someone else?"

Doing What You Already Do—On Your Own

Professionals and highly educated workers have always enjoyed maximum workplace and scheduling flexibility. Spinning off a portion of a salaried job to a free-lance basis, or simply developing a time-honored home-based free-lance job (like writing) holds financial promise while depending on a relatively limited roster of regular clients for income.

Compared to starting an actual business at home, free-lancing or consulting can be much less overwhelming. Because it's almost always a service business, there's no physical inventory to deal with. Having in-depth relationships with clients helps you know their needs intimately, smoothing communication and easing the way for sales of additional services.

The never-ending round of corporate layoffs is fueling demand for consultants and free-lancers. By hiring outside experts, a company can pay just for the expertise it needs, when it needs it. As well, high-performing corporate staffers who have been laid off frequently consult while they're job searching. Consequently, hiring outsiders is now perceived as smart management of corporate resources, paving the way for even greater acceptance of free-lancers.

Still, consultants and free-lancers have to prove themselves with each project they complete. Deadlines and clients' specifications set the parameters of projects. Frequently the projects require extended chunks of uninterrupted "think time," which can clash with your children's expectations of your availability.

You're the Product

Numerous skills can be adapted to free-lance work. Because you'll have to establish your credibility with new clients, it's best if you can document your ability with a portfolio of work and references from satisfied clients. If you have certifications from specialized training seminars or belong to hard-to-get-into professional groups, make sure they're listed on your résumé.

Consulting and free-lancing marketing strategies usually are most successful when you aim deep, not wide. Groom specialized skills and then aim for clients that need those skills. For instance, writing grant proposals is a very time consuming task for nonprofit organizations like museums, civic organizations, social service organizations, and ministries. If you've got a track record of writing proposals that result in the sought-after support, you can sell your expertise to nonprofits whose limited budgets may not stretch to accommodate a staff proposal writer. You don't have to have a background as a full-time proposal writer; demonstrating experience, and particularly results, should be enough for a client to give you a fair hearing.

Just-starting free-lancers and consultants frequently look to their immediate past employer as their first client. This is a common strategy because it usually works; you may want to line up the project before you leave. It's nearly always better to negotiate from a position of strength before you leave your job than to try to re-establish severed links after you leave.

If you're convinced that free-lancing or consulting is for you, write a proposal laying out all the ways that your current employer will benefit by breaking out projects and handing them off to you. You might point out the prorated savings of not paying benefits on your compensation, show how pulling the project out of the regular flow of work will improve its quality, and give a few examples of how internal resources can be reallocated more efficiently by jobbing out this project to you. (Maybe they'll hire you as a management consultant after your presentation!) Then show a step-by-step plan for getting the project done. Include a timetable showing points at which you'll check with your contact person to be sure that you're on target with the work to date.

After you have a solid relationship with a client, search for ways to take on additional projects with them. Many companies strongly prefer to work with a relatively small number of highly reliable free-lancers and consultants instead of constantly trying out new ones. This can make it difficult to get in the door, but it's a better deal for everybody involved over the long haul.

The Balancing Act

Talented, reliable free-lancers usually have more than enough work. Just ask Trish. Not only has she run a word processing and secretarial support service from her home since 1986, she also co-founded a metropolitan network for home workers whose computers are key to their operations. Network members refer work to each other, display their work at local business fairs, and pool resources to produce a member directory that's used as a marketing tool with local businesses.

Trish once conducted a seminar on desktop publishing and got ten thousand dollars worth of work as a direct result. In fact, her work struggles stem from too much work, not too little. Trish estimates that she works about sixty hours a week, much of it for her church and the network. She has a permanent part-time arrangement to provide secretarial services to a local executive who is herself a telecommuter. As well, Trish completes about twenty-five resumes per week at twenty-five dollars each.

"I love to work. It's tough for me not to work," she sighs. "Part of it is my personality. If I have undone work on my desk, I'm compelled to complete it. I'm getting better about it."

What Are You Worth?

One of the touchiest aspects of being a free-lancer or consultant is setting fees. You need to be competitive, yet you will only hurt yourself if you consistently underbid the going rate. Ask consultants with equivalent experience and in similar markets how they structure their fees. Extrapolate from this information a reasonable set of guidelines, including both hourly and by-the-project rates.

If you're not sure what a project rate should be, keep track of your hours for a typical project and use that as a basis. Another tactic is to charge a first-time client by the hour and negotiate project fees thereafter. That leaves you some wiggle room if you need to charge a particular client more for some reason; for instance, the client may routinely expect some extra research, or may be particularly difficult to deal with.

Expect that you'll overestimate some jobs, inadvertently giving yourself a nice windfall, and underestimate others, wiping out that windfall. Setting fees is essentially a process controlled by learned intuition. It will take some practice to get a feel for it.

Until you have long-term relationships with trusted clients, get all work agreements in writing. Standard consultant's contracts will spell out the related expenses for which you'll be reimbursed. It's also common to get one third of your expected fee when you sign the contract, one third when it's completed, and the remainder within thirty days of the project's delivery to the client.

Carving Out a Letter-perfect Niche

One of the best parts of free-lancing and consulting is that it allows a great deal of potential for personal and creative experimentation and growth. Without employees or a big list of customers depending on you, you can carve out time to pursue tangents that may or may not result in an immediate profit.

After getting degrees in journalism and art history, Roann finally came to grips with the fact that she felt called—almost compelled—to pursue fine art as a career. For years, she had been fascinated by calligraphy and had taken it up as a hobby. Soon it became a passion.

"God has given me this gift. When I don't use it, I'm one of the most unhappy people in the world. I struggle with 'What is the place of such a finely tuned art form in the Body of Christ?' It's not like saving souls," she confesses. "But when people see the Christian work I've done, it really speaks to them. It's an expression from the heart of God."

With her husband's full support, she invested in the pens, papers, drawing table, and classes that she would need to "go pro."

"I just decided that this is what I love to do, so I was going to go for it," she says. "We think of it as a ministry. This is my way to bless people."

Initially, Roann approached a local shop specializing in calligraphy supplies and mass-produced plaques, mugs, and other decorative items. In exchange for creating signs for the store, the manager put Roann's cards at the cash register and referred requests for custom work to her. She charged twenty-five to thirty dollars for an unmatted 8½-by-11 piece with ten to twenty words.

Though Roann didn't have any particular business plan in mind, it was a shrewd move. Soon she had enough work from referrals to fill her portfolio; better yet, her reputation was spreading.

Her next major break came when she sent her portfolio with some friends who were visiting an abbey that supported itself through producing and marketing art prints and greeting cards. The buyer there commissioned Roann to start a line of cards. After he approves the text she has developed, she creates accompanying art.

"I'm not a great greeting card writer," says Roann, who frequently runs to the public library in search of just the right quotation. "I'll just think about it and think about it. I mean, after 'Happy Birthday,' what else is there to say?"

Now, Roann has worked for several other producers and distributors of Christian cards, calendars, posters, and framed prints. Her goal is to earn twenty-five dollars an hour. She generally achieves that with the cards (despite her frequent writer's block), but gives herself leeway on the prints and posters to enjoy the process with less regard for the time.

She works around the schedule of her two preschool daughters. They are sometimes allowed in her basement studio, but because of the potential for major messes, she tries to work only when they are asleep or in her husband's charge.

Eventually, Roann wants to explore more artistic techniques, branch out into design, and experiment with various production methods. All that will have to wait, she believes, until her children are older. "I have a very nice set-up," she says. "All I need now is time."

❖ 7 ❖

Telecommuting, or Taming Technology

SOMETIMES LISA STILL finds herself surprised to be working at home. "I hadn't thought it was possible," says the twenty-nine-year-old electronic design engineer. "I thought I'd have to pay my dues for another ten years to be able to do something like this."

An employee of a small telecommunications technology design firm, Lisa telecommutes from her second-floor apartment. The back porch of the vintage apartment has been converted to a small workshop. She has her computer work station, tables, and myriad bins filled with bits and pieces of wires, connectors, and other paraphernalia needed to build prototypes.

Lisa's big chance came at a time when she was already considering how to adapt her career to accommodate a child. A former boss was starting his own company and wanted her to join the team. In order to take the job, she had to turn down an equally lucrative position with a bigger, more prestigious firm.

Being faced with the concrete offer forced Lisa and her husband Mike to "sit down and think about our long-term family goals. We really had to pray about it a lot," says Mike, adding that the input of close friends helped the couple clarify their objectives.

Before accepting the position, Lisa talked with her employer specifically about their desire to start a family and adapting to that with part-time hours. "After praying for a week, I felt I might need to take the risk to achieve my long-term goals," she relates.

Her employer pays travel expenses for the frequent meetings

and conventions that Lisa attends. The company also assisted with purchasing her home office equipment. Files, schematics, and project specifications are sent by overnight delivery or fax. She negotiated a full-time salary and complete benefit package.

To solidify her position, Lisa spent long hours strengthening her value to the company. She's now the resident expert in certain engineering subspecialties and even trains new engineers long-distance. However, she did turn down an offer to become an engineer manager because it was incompatible with her goals.

Lisa's hours, like those of any engineer, have always fluctuated according to the project she's currently working on. She worked full time, 8:00 A.M. to 5:00 P.M., for more than four years. Since baby Nicholas arrived, she has cut back to a part-time schedule, which varies from ten to twenty hours a week.

"My day is fragmented. When it's Nicholas's naptime, I try to work, but how much can I get done? Some days, it feels manageable. Other days I feel like it's not easy, but it's better than putting him in child care," she says. "When I'm with him I'm thinking of a work problem. And when I'm working I'm thinking, Now when did he last eat?

"I'm learning to adapt to constant change as a parent. It's the totally different nature of the two things I'm doing all day. I have to get my mind focused on all this electrical stuff and then I go back and make baby talk. I just have to make sure I'm saying the right thing to the right person."

While Lisa was settling in to her at-home work routine, Mike was examining his own career options. For about a year, he had a telecommuting position selling advertising space to marketers wanting to reach Christian pastors and church decision makers. That experience, plus some insight from a career counselor, convinced Mike that his personality and life values meshed well with a permanent at-home career. Self-evaluation revealed that security and family life were as important to him as the career itself and entrepreneurship. Money and prestige were trailing factors.

"Life-style integration turned out to be most important to me," he says. "Then came creativity and working by myself or in small groups."

In one way, the timing couldn't have been worse. Lisa had just gone to part-time hours, and Mike was unemployed. Their household income plummeted 75 percent.

"The hard part was not taking the first thing that came along," he says. Ironically, he ended up buying the exact media properties that he'd worked for before. Now, though, he reports to himself.

Lisa and Mike share housework (the laundry room is near his basement office) and keep each other accountable. Mike also gets together with another man who has a similar work and life-style to share ideas and figure out how to measure success.

"A lot of times I think, Oh, I really don't want to make calls this morning. I think I'll play a game of computer golf," says Mike with a grin. "Then you look at the budget and realize that unless you sell something, there's going to be trouble."

Both Mike and Lisa had to come to grips with their tendency to hole up in their office and home and withdraw from the world. They push themselves to get out socially and pursue friendships with people in their neighborhood and church.

"We need to feel like we're not on a little island," says Mike. "I go out for coffee and doughnuts at a local greasy spoon every day just to see faces. When I worked in an office, I went for walks at lunch so I could be alone!"

When the Process Is Your Product

Engineers, word processors, and other people with information-driven jobs are likely to find that it's relatively easy to transplant their careers to a home office. After all, they spend much of their days glued to a computer screen anyway. Moving the site of the computer doesn't have much of a material effect on the mechanics of performing the job.

Less obvious are the ways in which technology is making it feasible for previously office-bound jobs to be converted to telecommuting positions. Word processing and other clerical support positions, researching, phone sales, computer programming, transcribing, and accounting can all be performed via a personal computer and a modem link. Some major corporations are experimenting with having catalog sales reps and reservation agents work from home but on-line with the company computer. Even the IRS has a pilot project for seeing if agents might be more efficient (one would hope, more humane as well) working from home.

Not Everybody's Doing It—But They're Thinking about It

Telecommuting has caught the attention of government bureaucrats and community planners as well. The federal Clean Air Act, which aims to reduce air pollution in part through reshaping commuting patterns, allows corporations to comply with the regulations by establishing telecommuting programs. In California and Arizona, where similar state legislation is already being enforced, the number of telecommuters has soared as a direct result. A think tank in Denver called the Center for the New West is developing plans to help rural communities upgrade their telecommunications infrastructures so that they can attract "Lone Eagles."

According to the center, Lone Eagles typically are self-employed information workers and professionals. They're attracted to the laid-back small town and rural life-style; all they need to set up shop is their equipment. They represent a clean, nearly invisible way to boost the local economy; according to LINK Resources, a research firm, the income of the average telecommuting household is $50,160. The Center for the New West estimates that there are about nine million home-based workers who are or want to be Lone Eagles.

LINK Resources reports that currently there are about 6.6 million telecommuters; their ranks are growing at about a 20 percent annual rate. But as impressive as those statistics are, they won't do you much good until you become one of them.

Having Your Cake and Eating It Too

Telecommuting offers some of the advantages of working from home with much of the security of being employed. Full-time telecommuters routinely have the same benefits as in-office workers. The tradeoff comes with the imposition of certain hours and deadlines, which usually are set by your supervisor. Though telecommuters usually go in to the home office on a regular basis, Lisa and Mike's struggles with isolation are typical.

A major hitch in converting a current job to a telecommuting position is the fact that many managers are not sure how they will be able to supervise you. "Management by walking around" does not apply when your subordinate's desk is forty miles away. Even if company policy officially encourages telecommuting, it's best if you have a supportive boss with whom you have a solid track record.

Work up a proposal outlining how the job would function long-distance. Cover as many specifics as you can; for instance, would you still come in to the Monday morning project update and strategy sessions? Is there a clerical worker on-site who can be in charge of faxing you routine company memos so that you're not out of the loop on company policy? Will you be included in training opportunities and professional conferences?

Anticipate some issues that may feel uncomfortable to your boss. How will you report to him or her? How will performance reviews be handled?

Gone but Not Forgotten

As you're doing this, consider ways that you can compensate for the fact that you won't be there in person, yet are still part of the team. How will you demonstrate commitment to the job to your boss, to coworkers?

For instance, say they are afraid they will interrupt your dinner if they call just after 5:00 P.M. to relay a message from a client in a different time zone. As considerate as that seems at the time, it can boomerang the next day if you're the only person without the crucial information. The way you handle relatively minor situations like that will make an impression that will work for you (if you're gracious and cooperative) or against you (if your tone of voice makes it clear that you don't appreciate the intrusion).

When you present your telecommuting plan to your superiors, address start-up issues such as what kind of office you'll have and who will pay for your equipment. According to LINK, 90 percent of technology purchases made to support telecommuters are made by the individuals themselves. Your employer may allow you to bring home your computer, but things like a fax machine, copier, and other equipment will come out of your pocket.

Negotiate as to who will cover ongoing expenses such as a dedicated phone line, subscriptions to professional journals, and office supplies. Keep in mind that other communications technologies that initially seem frivolous may become necessary. In order to be accessible to their coworkers and supervisor at all times, some telecommuters install car phones, wear beepers, or carry portable phones around with them. That way, there's no excuse not to call when their input is needed at an impromptu meeting.

Show and Tell

Actually seeing your home office will probably help your supervisor in two ways: it will show him or her that you've invested in the appropriate physical set-up, and it helps him or her visualize how the workday will run.

Once you've made the proposal to switch to telecommuting, suggest that it start on a trial basis. This will be a good face saver if it doesn't work out. As well, it's harder to reject a change that's couched in terms of "let's try it and see." Be prepared to adjust along the way.

Then track your progress. Document your efficiency so that you can prove that you're just as good at your job as you were before you moved home. If you're better, say so. Perhaps you find that you actually get more done once you're not distracted by water-cooler gatherings and the doughnut cart. If that's the case, and your supervisor trusts you, make a pitch for either a shortened workday (in which you accomplish the same amount) or take on more work and position yourself for a promotion or raise.

If your supervisor has a sense of humor, hang a framed picture of him or her over your desk. Then have someone take a picture of you with your boss's picture. Frame it and give it to him or her so that you'll never be out of sight—or out of mind.

❖8❖

Reinventing the Traditional Workplace

IT TOOK SEVEN years of praying, but Elizabeth finally got the break she needed in her work schedule. It didn't come when she wanted it, but when it *had* to.

For over ten years, she'd been working a full nine-to-five work week in the editorial department of a monthly magazine covering the macho world of heavy construction equipment. After three years, she was promoted to managing editor, the position she still holds. At about the same time, she gave birth to her first child; four years later, she had her second.

"It was very hard for me to put the kids in day care. I prayed about it for a long time," she relates. The issue came to a head when her first child was approaching school age. She and her husband, a Christian counselor, wanted very much to homeschool their children. Elizabeth wrote a proposal to her company's management outlining her plan to work five days a week from 6:00 A.M. to 2:00 P.M. In essence, she was trying to shape a customized flextime schedule.

As reasonable as her request was, the fossilized group of corporate managers was petrified by the possibility of setting a precedent that—heaven forbid!—other employees might want for themselves.

"When they said no, my boss and I went down to the cafeteria to talk about it. I told him that my choices were to either keep working nine to five and be unhappy about it or quit. Well, he didn't want either of those. He offered me the option of working from home one-and-a-half days a week. We editors travel a lot, and we're always using our laptop computers to work on the road. So he was able to approve that.

"It's an informal thing that's been going on now for two years. I work the same number of hours, but I do it in fewer days. I feel very refreshed. I'm thrilled to be home with my kids for an additional day each week."

Squeezing a full workload into fewer days means that Elizabeth has had to reexamine her management style. Typically, her morning starts at 4:00 A.M. She exercises, has a devotional time, and spends a little time on personal projects. By 5:30 she's in the office, where she can spend several extremely productive hours before the rest of the staff arrive at 9:00. On her work-from-home days, she usually edits some stories or concentrates on some long-term planning. Her husband's work hours tend to be in the afternoons and evenings, so they are able to share homeschool and household responsibilities equitably.

Elizabeth credits the success of her ad hoc flextime to her excellent relationship with her immediate supervisor, the magazine's editor. Because their personalities, abilities, and preferences are complementary—in fact, nearly opposite—each happily recognizes the other's strengths.

"He doesn't bother me. He values me," she says. "He lets me manage the magazine."

In turn, she has adopted the same hands-off management style towards the staff she manages. The reporters handle their assignments with little input other than routine staff meetings. When she hired her own two assistants, one a production editor and the other a secretary/research assistant, Elizabeth deliberately chose independent self-starters who don't need lots of hand-holding and back-patting to get their jobs done.

In effect, her flextime arrangement has been invisible to the corporate managers because it hasn't affected day-to-day operations.

Elizabeth's home life is just as jam-packed. "We're scheduled to the max," she says. "Every day has to be planned out. We have a huge calendar in the kitchen where we write everything down, because the parent who schedules something may not be the one to do it."

She and her husband have had to pare down their out-of-home commitments to juggle their respective schedules. He has counseling appointments and related meetings in the afternoons, evenings, and on occasional Saturdays. Sundays are their one day to spend together as a family. As well, they try to take several family weekend getaways each year.

"We have to be sure we don't schedule things that are unimportant. We don't do a lot of things that people probably think we should," Elizabeth reflects.

For instance, she and her husband attend two of the three monthly meetings of the church small group to which they belong. Other than at birthdays and holidays, they don't entertain at home. Instead of spending an afternoon a week with a home-school support group, Elizabeth gets advice and support from several newsletters she subscribes to and from an informal network of family and church friends who also homeschool.

While many people might consider her situation ideal, Elizabeth draws a distinction between her career goals and her life objectives. While she likes her job and knows she's operating at peak efficiency there, she stresses that she has no overriding career aspirations. "I'm very content with my job," she says. "It's just where I want to be. The next step would require a lot of budgets and meetings and planning, and I don't want to do it. It's not where my gifts are."

More important, her job is just one piece of the overall calling that she and her husband believe God has on their lives. As a Christian counselor specializing in homosexuality and AIDS victims, her husband will probably not ever make a significant amount of money. In fact, Elizabeth's salary accounts for 65 percent of their household earnings and all of their retirement, health, and insurance benefits. In effect, her willingness to work long hours outside the home is an investment in his ministry—a vision they hold jointly. She's also concentrating on maintaining a God-centered household in which to rear her children.

"I feel that women should try to stay home," she says. "I'd quit in a minute if I could. But I haven't had that option. Financially, it hasn't been possible."

Instead of hoping for a day that may not come, Elizabeth has directed her energies into being both an excellent mother and an excellent employee. "I prayed seven years for this. And I still pray constantly. I feel this is something God gave me. God will change situations when you least expect it."

Mommy Track—Freedom Trail or Dead End?

Flexible work arrangements burst on the corporate scene in the late 1980s. Most companies are still experimenting with various permutations of flextime, compressed work weeks, job sharing, and career-track part-time work. The tidal waves of publicity that have accompanied a few corporations' more family-friendly policies have helped to make it seem like a new norm. Industry leaders like Arthur Anderson, IBM, and Aetna Insurance have received bushels of kudos for their progressive flexible policies. Even the federal government, rarely a bastion of innovative management, is getting on the bandwagon. Federal bureaucracies in and around traffic-clogged Washington, D.C., are trying out various flextime, telecommuting, and job sharing options.

There is evidence that corporate America is beginning to loosen up. Catalyst is a research firm that focuses on issues of women and work. According to a survey it commissioned, 87.8 percent of companies offer part-time work; 77 percent offer flextime; 47.9 percent offer job sharing; and 35 percent offer flexplace (working from home).

Unfortunately, the perception of dramatic change has preceded the reality. In truth, most companies are tiptoeing into the area of flexible work arrangements, trying to do enough to retain very valuable employees but not so much that entrenched managers feel threatened. That's why Elizabeth's situation is typical. Her publishing company is one of the stingiest and stodgiest in its field; yet she and her very supportive manager made an end run around official corporate policy.

Sometimes You Can't Take It with You

Some people and some jobs simply can't be adapted to at-home work. Fortunately, the people who hold these jobs are often the ones who thrive on the interaction and activity of an office and are actually more productive there. If you're loathe to leave the office, or if you have a position that you like and are invested in that absolutely requires a physical presence on the job (managing is a prime example), you may be better off redesigning your current position than working from home and hating it.

Another reason to stay in the corporate world is to maintain a minimum level of health and other benefits. It's certainly much easier to go back to full-time work than it is to quit altogether and try to reenter several years later.

However, a custom-paved career track is not without potholes. Unsupportive bosses and coworkers who resent your "light load" are probably the most difficult roadblocks to get around. Once negotiated, your hours and situation may not be flexible, aggravating conflicts with family commitments. You'll still have to arrange for child care. Work-related incidental expenses, like wardrobe, dry cleaning, and household help, may be scaled down but probably not eliminated. Analyze your financial situation carefully to see if your actual income will be worth the effort.

A No-Lose Proposition

As with telecommuting, the key to negotiating a flexible work schedule is to position it as win-win. You'll need to think of it in terms of how your company will benefit by keeping you on in your changed capacity. The experience of companies that do offer flexible arrangements is encouraging. Catalyst research indicates that employee retention is a major motivation for 64 percent of companies that use flexible work arrangements; 70 percent of survey respondents reported that flexible work arrangements had a positive effect on employee morale; and 65 percent said that employees on flexible schedules are more productive.

The longer you've been with a company, the more they have to lose when you leave. Your knowledge of the company's goals, culture, and procedures are an important asset. Companies that are trying to stay mean and lean need to make every employee count. If you have survived corporate shakeouts, you are probably in a very good negotiating position.

A basic first step is to analyze the predominant culture at your company. Try to determine if the managers truly reward results, or if they tend to focus only on the people in their path—those who are there only because of the corporate structure. Try to find a supervisor whose focus is getting the work done, not micromanaging schedules.

Next, find out directly from the human resources department just what your company's official policies are. Find out if other employees have fashioned arrangements similar to the one you want, and interview them as to the pros and cons of the situation.

Ask the human resources folks if they're getting—and filling—requests from various departments to hire executive or technical temporary workers. If that's the case, it could signal both a need for as-needed workers and an acceptance of them.

Then consider how you'll use your time differently under the scenario you want to pursue. If you want to work part time, keep in mind that research indicates that half-time workers usually accomplish 70 percent of a full-time load in their allotted time. Because they're in the office less, they shake off corporate time-wasters and dig right into the work.

Build on Your Success

The primary selling points of your proposal will probably be your current (and, you hope, continued) value to the company and the advantages of your adjusted work situation to your boss. Lower overhead, your own loyalty and commitment to the company ("Where else could I get such a deal as you're going to make me?"), and continuity of the portions of your job that you'll keep are key points.

Be sure to underscore how these ongoing benefits fit into the company's overall goals. Emphasize your flexibility, too, to come in on off-days to important meetings, fill in during busy periods and during coworkers' vacations, and so on. Make it easy for your manager to say yes; suggest that you try out the flexible schedule for a certain number of months and then evaluate.

Once you've successfully negotiated your ideal work arrangement, carry on as usual. If you adopt an overly grateful or apologetic attitude, or suddenly start spouting to coworkers about all the wonderful things you get to do in your newly expanded family time, you may get glares instead of grins. Their feelings toward your arrangement can make it or break it, particularly if you are working part time, or if you are job-sharing. In either case, you'll be depending on them to keep you informed about what happened when you were gone. (Job-sharers need to work out their own communication system, perhaps overlapping for a morning, so that they aren't always playing catch-up.)

It's absolutely essential that you meticulously document your accomplishments.

"I expect to get raises," says Elizabeth. She keeps a log of her magazine's record of meeting all deadlines and of the additional projects—research issues, for instance—that she heads.

When review time rolls around, you need to be able to protect your newly staked-out turf. If your manager is bothered by coworkers' charges that you're not pulling your weight, you don't have to get defensive. Instead, you can set the record straight with your log book. This will be particularly important if your supervisor tends to measure accomplishments by "face time," or how frequently he sees his employees, instead of by objective results.

Determine Your Bottom Line

If one of your goals is reducing your hours, you can expect that your salary and benefits will be prorated from your full-time salary. A general rule of thumb is that you can make a strong case for maximum benefits with your contribution in proportion to those of full-time employees, if you are working at least thirty hours a week.

If you work less than that, expect to pay proportionately more for your benefits than full-timers. Employees working less than twenty hours a week don't get many choices when it comes to fringe benefits.

View the elements of compensation as bargaining chips. Trade, say, a slightly lower salary for a more generous benefits package. If flexibility is your main goal, offer to forfeit benefits altogether to work at home for half of the week. If the company is under financial pressure, offer to trade reduced hours for a promised raise.

The Down Side of Flex

Setting up an ad-hoc flexible situation with a coworker or sympathetic boss can have its disadvantages, too, as Rachel discovered.

A territory manager for a department store cosmetics firm, Rachel had spent a hectic two years hiring and training salespeople, creating and staging promotions, and analyzing retail trends and consumers' whimsies. It wasn't the kind of job that she wanted to keep up after her son was born, so she didn't.

Several months after she left, a former coworker asked her to participate in an informal job-share. The coworker loved the creative aspects of managing her territory, but she hated the accounting paperwork and administrative work. Rachel happened to like that part of the job.

They agreed that the coworker would ship out reams of paperwork to Rachel's house on an as-needed basis; Rachel would make it a top priority and turn it around immediately, for thirteen dollars an hour. The coworker had a discretionary fund for paying models, demonstrators, and other temporary workers. She used some of those funds to pay Rachel.

Because Rachel had been through several buying cycles, she knew what to expect. "It started by my doing clerical work, but it evolved into my actually doing the orders with real responsibility," Rachel says. "The whole situation was great for me. I love to work with numbers; she didn't. The things I did not like to do, she did like. It broke down very naturally."

The arrangement worked smoothly for three years. Then Rachel's former coworker abruptly left the company. Because Rachel's job was based on the relationship and was not with the cosmetics company, the work disappeared.

Now she regrets having put all her eggs in one basket. "I'd still be doing it if I'd maintained relationships in the business," she says.

Starting Over

Sometimes you can't negotiate, beg, or borrow the flexibility you need at your current company. Or, if you've been out of the work force for several years, you may feel that you aren't in a position to start out with a flexible arrangement.

Don't despair. Package up your proposal outlining the benefits to an employer and take it on the road. It's harder to get a flexible job than it is to rearrange your current position, but it can be done.

"A lot of women use their time at home to rethink their career path and make changes," says Martha Bowen, past president of FEMALE (Formerly Employed Mothers at the Leading Edge, a national association of at-home mothers).

They have to reestablish their credentials, perhaps by rejoining associations and attending meetings, doing pro bono work for nonprofit groups, and taking classes to brush up their skills. Free-lance work that fills in gaps in a résumé will make a big difference.

Big companies that pride themselves on their progressive work/family policies may lend an open ear to hiring someone with a flexible schedule to begin with. Don't overlook small- and medium-sized companies. Frequently they can't offer top salaries, but they may be so eager to get an experienced, motivated employee that they're more than willing to bend on the specifics of your schedule and work place.

The best time to start this process is years before you need to. If you are working full time and are beginning to consider how you might structure your career when you have children, need to care for aged parents, or just want more free time, start planning now. Your track record with your employer will be your most valuable asset when you sit down to negotiate.

Follow the progress of people who have successfully arranged the kind of flexible position you want. Find out what's happening in the rest of the company. Perhaps a manager in another department will be more sympathetic to your goals; it may be worth it to get transferred to that department even if you have to complete some retraining or shift jobs to qualify.

Above all, remember that you can invest in your future, starting now.

·9·

Getting Started

WHEN IT COMES to working from home, what you do is more important than where you do it. Your clients and customers will come back to you because of the excellent service, unique products, and value you offer, regardless of whether you're located in a sparsely furnished spare bedroom or a teak-paneled corner office.

However, even the most loyal and understanding clients and customers can get annoyed when a three year old answers the phone and they can't get the kid to "go get Mommy." Successfully working from home means that you can't let your location—an advantage for you personally—be a drawback for your clientele.

The following tips for successfully organizing a home office are only to get you started. Pick and choose the ones that seem most applicable to your situation and ignore the rest. I'm sure that as you develop and refine your own home-work style, you'll come up with solutions to specific problems that are far better than generic advice you'll read here or anywhere else.

Get Serious

The key word in the phrase "home-based business" is "business." Unless you are planning to lose money, set up your business by the books right from the start.

• Before you jump into your home business head first, assess your family's financial situation. At the back of this book are several basic worksheets for figuring out what it costs you to have a second income, how to figure your net worth, and how to estimate basic business start-up and ongoing expenses. Use these worksheets only for preliminary work; you'll need more sophisticated forms for your business plan and other projections.

• Regardless of the type of home-work you want to pursue, develop a business plan. If you don't have the discipline to do the plan, do you have the discipline to work from home? When you approach a banker or venture capitalist for funding, he will immediately want to scrutinize your business plan. Extend the same consideration to family and friends that you contact for start-up funds. Who knows—you might get so good at writing business plans that you end up doing that for a living!

• Discuss forms of business entities with your spouse, accountant, and, if needed, attorney. Sole proprietorships, partnerships, subchapter-S corporations, corporations—each form of legal organization and ownership has its own drawbacks and advantages. The implications of each for personal and corporate liabilities, tax regulations, and business planning vary widely. Research the implications of each of these ownership structures for your state and then consult a lawyer or tax attorney to decide which is right for your venture.

• As soon as you have settled on a corporate name, register it with the secretary of state's office. As well, don't procrastinate in filing for trademark status when you have developed a name, logo, graphics, and other proprietary marks for your product or service. You can get in trouble for inadvertently "stealing" a name that's already in use by another business. Nor do you want someone else usurping your brand names, graphics, and so on.

• Carefully consider your company name. If you're a one-person shop, don't try to sound like a big conglomerate. Potential clients will only feel deceived. Tailor the name of your company or business to appeal to the market you're trying to reach. Avoid using a general term like "consultant"—zero in on your niche with a more specific term like project manager or researcher.

• Establish a separate business checking account. Don't mingle business and personal funds, even if they are separate on paper.

• Comply from the beginning with the state and federal tax codes that apply to the type of business structure you decide on. Cash flow will be affected by IRS regulations regarding prepayment of estimated income taxes and other fun formulas. The penalties for ignorance are stiff. Consult your accountant.

• Set up a bookkeeping system for keeping track of incidental as well as major expenses. Even little things like tolls and mileage add up fast. You must be able to document each of your business expenses, so establish a system for doing so at the beginning. Ask your accountant to recommend a small business software package. Having your records in order will save you time, hassle, and money when it comes time to prepare your corporate tax return.

• Remember that in order to qualify for a home office deduction, your office must be used exclusively and regularly for the primary functions of your business. A desktop publishing service set up in a finished basement counts; a crafter's workshop/office probably doesn't, because the principal business (selling) takes place off-premises (at crafts fairs).

Keep a log of all activities and client meetings that take place in your office to support your "primary business function" claim; also hold on to evidence of business mail addressed to your home. When in doubt, call your accountant.

• If you hire your children for any significant amount of money, you will have to pay taxes on their income just as you would for any other employee.

• Check with the local branch of the Labor Department to make sure that your crafts business doesn't violate any industrial home worker laws. The convoluted regulations primarily ban assembly of ladies' garments and jewelry, but don't assume anything. You could get busted for operating something as innocuous as a small teddy bear assembly line.

• Don't assume that your homeowner's or renter's insurance policy covers your business equipment, materials, and inventory. If it doesn't, get proper coverage. Do you need a home security system?

• If you do need to buy essential medical, dental, and life insurance, inquire at your local chamber of commerce, professional association, or regional business advocacy association about their small business group policies.

The Technological Convolution

Now is the time to abandon all those self-deprecating jokes about being computer-illiterate. Make technology your slave. You'll be more efficient, more professional, and you can amaze your kids by photocopying their hands at home.

• Poll people in your line of work to see what combinations of hardware and software they recommend. You'll want to be working on the industry standard, or at least something compatible with it.

Is your work based on technology (computer programming, desktop publishing) or supported by technology? For instance, reporting is based on personal skills—researching, interviewing, and ability to write. The computer enhances my ability to get the job done, but my job isn't inherently dependent on my ability to do it. (It's actually the opposite—the faster my computer goes, the slower I think.)

Exactly how you use your technology will help you determine how much technological support you need.

• Expect to spend at least two thousand dollars for a basic computer set-up, including printer and elementary software. Consider buying through a small business association. If you are a computer novice, hire a small business computer consultant to advise you on the right configuration of software, hardware, and peripherals you'll need.

• Always, *always* back up your work on a separate computer disk. Establish an off-site facility (it doesn't have to be fancy—your mom's house will do) for long-term storage of archival disks. If disaster strikes your home office, at least you'll have copies of your programs, data bases, and other vital files and information.

• Install separate electrical lines for each of your major pieces of equipment. Don't forget the surge protectors.

• Install at least one business phone and preferably two. Keep one line free for incoming calls and use the other to make calls. That way, you'll minimize the chance that a customer or client will get an annoying busy signal. A lost call is lost business.

• Have a dedicated phone line for your fax and/or modem.

• Consider carefully what kind of phone answering system will make life easiest. In the past couple of years, local phone companies have discovered the home office trend. Now you can get a voice-mail system that sounds as sophisticated as any corporate system you'll do battle with. Answering machines have evolved too; you can get them to handle two lines or with separate voice mailboxes for employees, primary clients, or family members. You can still get the low-tech, high-touch option—engaging an answering service that features live people.

How will you be using the answering system? Will it be a high-tech substitute for the refrigerator door; a clearinghouse for family messages? If customers will be leaving long, detailed orders, you need to invest in a sophisticated machine that features a way to save messages permanently. With a phone machine, you can screen calls; you can't with a voice mail system.

• If you spend a lot of time on the phone, get a headset. It will save neck strain and it looks cool.

• If you must have a portable phone, get the best quality one you can possibly afford. Don't risk losing sales or irritating clients because they can't hear what you're saying over a static-y connection.

• Resist the temptation to buy lots of state-of-the-art machines and pieces of equipment right off the bat. Make do with the local copy center's fax for awhile if you need to, until you see how much you really will use a fax machine. Conserve your start-up capital for marketing and operations.

The One with the Messiest Desk Wins

Here's one thing you won't have to do at your home office: straighten it up for visitors. Most client meetings should take place at the client's office, anyway. When that's not appropriate, meet at a restaurant. Other alternatives where you can rent a meeting room include small-business incubator buildings, airport business support centers, hotels, and high-quality municipal recreation centers. Forget libraries; meetings there have to be open to the public.

• Renting a post office box can help establish your status as a business; it also lets you pick up your mail whenever you want, instead of facing the deluge every day. However, private delivery services will not deliver to a post office box.

• Check out the amenities offered by the local small-business support center. You can lease a mail box, receive and send private deliveries like UPS and Federal Express, receive and send faxes, and take care of minor shipping needs without maintaining your own inventory of bags and boxes.

• See what minor business chores you can hire out that will lighten your load. Have a maid service or a child clean your office twice monthly. Contract with a telecommuting, home-based secretarial service to churn out routine correspondence.

• Develop personal personnel policies. Schedule breaks throughout the day; set up a reward system for yourself.

• Keep a tickler file. This is a hanging file with a folder for each day of the month. Put papers, bills, forms, and other notes that you'll need for each day in the appropriate file. Store inactive files in the basement or garage.

Home–Office Improvement

Don't you hate those home-decorating magazine articles about home offices? Most of them include at least one plan for converting an unused closet into an efficient little profit center. Puh-leeze! Who ever heard of an extra closet?

• Don't buy into the lie that your home office is an extension of your personality and as such deserves royal treatment. Start with adequate furniture and upgrade only when you have the money and other family goals are being met. Put your money not into things that will look good, but things that will work well.

• The one exception to the above: your desk chair. Get the most comfortable, ergonomically correct one you can afford. Expect to spend as much as one thousand dollars. Your back will thank you.

• Shop for used office furniture.

• Make your office as separate from the rest of the house as possible. Having it on a separate floor or devoting one room to the office makes it much easier to shut the door and ignore it when you're not working. If you don't have a spare room, at least pull a screen or room divider across your work area when you're done for the day.

• For the sake of your marriage, don't put your office in your bedroom. It's an invasion of privacy. Your ardor for both work and intimacy will be dampened.

• Are you a sloppy worker, thriving on clutter and bins of papers, correspondence and files in plain view, and Rolodexes helter-skelter? Or are you one of those who actually cleans off her desk after each workday? Either way, get the filing systems that you need.

• Work from home for several months before spending big bucks on an office addition or remodeling. First, you may find that you don't want to work from home. Second, you'll learn a lot about your work/life-style preferences when you do it; third, you may not make as much money as you think and you don't want to be hamstrung by debt right from the start.

The Littlest Entrepreneurs

The best time to introduce children to your home business is before they're born. Nancy (from chapter 6) believes that it's easier for a child to grow up with a home office than have the situation imposed on him or her. Be that as it may, most kids will have to adjust. The degree to which a home-based business will reduce child care needs depends less on the kind of business than on your personality and expectations.

Other important factors are your children's ages and personalities. It's not that difficult to free-lance with a cooperative baby around. When that child is a rambunctious eighteen-month-old, all energy and no common sense, you may be staying up late to accomplish what you used to get done during afternoon naps.

• What is your family's approach to discipline? What kind of consequences will be meted out when your kids violate your rules about invading your work space?

• What's your preference: to be near the center of the action, ready to answer the front door, resolve kids' fights over which video to watch, and keep an eye on dinner on the stove—or do you prefer to be isolated, out of the path of daily life?

• Decide with your spouse how you will handle unwarranted interruptions of your dedicated work time, and what the consequences will be for offenders. Be consistent.

• Use a system to indicate your "interruptability level": a red flag for no disruptions; a yellow flag means come in but be quiet and respectful; a green flag means you can engage in casual conversation.

• Establish firm rules for phone etiquette. I recommend banning children from the using the business phone altogether.

• Likewise, have clear guidelines as to who may use the computer and when. Make sure your kids are adept at the software so they can save and close your files and open their own.

Are you willing to let them share your computer with their friends? If you subscribe to an on-line database, make sure the kids understand how much it costs to use the service. Establish limits and have them pay for the service themselves after a certain dollar amount has been used up.

• Baby-proof your office. Keep staplers, letter openers, scissors, paper punches, sharp-edged filing systems, copier and printer toner, and other potentially lethal items well out of reach. Keep phone and electrical cords short to avoid tangling.

• Find a child care provider who is willing to let you experiment with the days and hours that kids are in child care so you can hit on the right arrangement. Make sure that the peace and quiet you buy when the kids are with the sitter is converted directly into increased efficiency.

• Trade child care with another home working mother.

• Hire a young teen to come over after school and take your preschoolers to the park, make Play-Dough, and otherwise romp around from 3:00 to 5:30 P.M.

• Have a box of scrap paper, blunt scissors, tape, and washable markers in a corner of the office available for quiet play.

• When you have to take an important call and your toddler is facing you, poised on the edge of a temper tantrum, try: handing him little bits of tape, one by one; giving him a whole pad of Post-It notes; letting him play at the computer keyboard (in a benign file); giving him correction fluid and colored paper to paint with; letting him wash the windows and computer screen with premoistened glass cleaner wipes; giving him a long, long strip of blank computer mailing labels that he can stick all over your furniture; pulling out the bottom drawer of your desk and letting him stand on it and glare at you.

• Encourage your kids to develop business plans of their own.

The Personal Touch

When you represent yourself, a positive first impression is crucial. If you only need a couple of "power suits" in your home-work wardrobe, make them knockouts. This is especially important if you're expanding your business and meeting lots of potential clients.

• Do you need to polish your skills in letter writing, speaking, conducting meetings, or managing press interviews? If so, track down classes or seminars that will help bring you up to speed.

• I've found that most home business people have more in common with other people in their fields (mail order sales, their profession, etc.) than they do with other people who work from home. Working from home is a tenuous thing to have in common because people's specific arrangements, philosophies of work, and motivations vary so widely. You may find it meaningful to join a support group of other home workers whose stage in life is similar to yours. However, don't kid yourself that it will be a major networking venue. You'll have to count on professional and business associations to see and be seen.

Faith into Action

Don't let all the details of starting and running a home business paralyze you. It is a lot of work, but you are not the only one doing it. I hope that your home-work venture will be led by the Lord as clearly as Evelyn's.

After working for a major international insurance company as a computer programmer for eight years, she was laid off. She was determined not to go on unemployment, yet was flummoxed as to what kind of job she should purse.

"I prayed, 'God, please show me how to make a living,' " she says. "That's how I know this thing is God-driven." Two weeks later, Evelyn saw a television show demonstration of how to make decorative dolls from twisted paper. "I thought, I could do that," she says.

At the store buying the materials, Evelyn was struck by how the brown, gold, and red hues were similar to those used in traditional African dress. She made her doll wearing an African-inspired outfit, and it was an immediate hit with her friends and local shop owners. Evelyn's line of African pride dolls are now being carried by ethnic-oriented shops around the country, represented by an enthusiastic corps of friends and relatives. The eighteen-inch dolls retail for twenty to fifty dollars, depending on the detail of their outfits.

"I didn't know I had all this artistic ability," she says. "I was just having fun. I thought a business required receipts and marketing and then it wouldn't be fun anymore."

Actually, it's turning out to be quite a bit of fun. Evelyn is now negotiating with one of the country's biggest manufacturers and mass marketers of porcelain figurines. If all goes well, her concept of African-American heritage decorative dolls will be interpreted on a grand scale.

"I was giving away the dolls in the beginning and still wondering where I was going to get money," she says. "Then it dawned on me that my prayers were being answered. So I tell people, after you pray, you've got to be quiet and listen."

·10·

Get a Grip on It!

THE MORE YOU research work trends, be they home-based or flexible arenas of work, and the home-work life-style, the better prepared you will be to make smart decisions.

Use the resources in this chapter as jumping-off points to delve into the specifics of the type of business and work situation you want to pursue.

For instance, if you're interested in buying a home decorating franchise, start by reading a general book on franchising to see if it's the kind of corporate set-up that's congruent with your ethical beliefs and preferred business practices. You'll also get an idea as to what kind of financial commitment and effort are likely to be required to start, and what you can expect from a franchising company.

Then use on-line data bases, industry trade journals (in this case, *Home Furnishings Daily* is the standard), trade association literature, and other public or university library resources to get lots of background information on the industry. Find out about established business practices, sources of raw materials, typical distribution and marketing methods, ongoing training for franchisees, and general trends (is demand growing? shrinking? hard hit by economic downturns or recession-resistant? dependent on only a few resources?).

Determine the barriers to entry; i.e., how hard is it to get started? Are there many competitors or few? Don't forget to analyze the contents of your own market area's Yellow Pages. Find out how many competitors you have and how well-established they are. Are some of the market leaders launching aggressive expansion plans?

(You don't want your new business to get caught in a slugfest between two industry giants!)

See what niches aren't filled. Search trade and business journals and local papers for stories on the status of the decorating industry locally. As you research, develop your business plan.

Find out how pricing is set and whether or not discounts are common. Figure out just where the profit is in the business (commission? mark-up? distribution?), how much you'll have to charge to make money, and where your anticipated pricing structure fits in the industry norms. If you think your prices will be high, what will make your services worth the premium? If you want to target the low end of the market, ask yourself why no one else is doing so.

Figure out how you'll deliver your goods and services. In person? Through employees? Via mail or private shipping service? Electronically? What percent of market share and sales volume can you expect to attract, and what competitive advantage do you have to accomplish that?

Once you've thoroughly scoped out the lay of the land, both generally and locally, turn your attention to setting up a business plan that incorporates both your research and sound financial planning practices. Use one of the guidebooks listed below or enlist the help of a local small business group.

If conservatively estimated numbers indicate that you'll be able to turn a profit within a reasonable amount of time, take your proposal to a banker, CPA, or small business advisor for a critique.

Throughout this entire process, be sure to pray that God will lead you to divine appointments. I am not above praying for a friendly librarian! Also, pray that you'll connect with some other Christian business people in the same field who can give you solid, biblically based advice.

Don't be paralyzed by the start-up process. It is a lot of work, but it's only the prelude to the real job—launching your home business. Fill your tank, so to speak, with knowledge, and pray for wisdom. When it's time to shift from park to drive, you'll be drawing on your full tank to carry you through the first hectic months or business cycles.

Once your momentum is established, settle on the handful of business journals and associations that you'll need to keep the flow of information coming. The mix that you find most beneficial will depend on your work style and field. Experiment to find the combination that most efficiently meets your needs for business information and a "support" function. Probably you will prefer to get two or three general business newspapers or magazines, one or two specific to your field, and perhaps one "work style" resource.

For instance, as a writer I need a constant flow of news, analysis, and information on marketing my ideas. As editor of a travel newsletter, I needed to know what was happening in the world of newsletter publishing and with travel trends. As a home worker, I need personal support and a sense of not being all alone.

To address these varied needs, I read two daily newspapers, one national and one metropolitan. I subscribe to about ten national monthly business magazines. I read the newsletter of the Newsletter Association. I'm not much interested in deserting my family at the end of day to attend networking cocktail parties, so I network during the work week, usually over lunch. Fortunately, I have a variety of home-working friends, and I'm in constant contact with various editors and staff. Finally, my entrepreneurially minded husband provides emotional support and excellent advice.

Your mix may look much different. You may subscribe to one general business magazine and three publications (including association material) related to your field, and attend both home-work support and local chamber of commerce meetings. At the home-work support meetings, you may develop personal friends with children the same age as yours. At the chamber meetings, you may meet potential customers, touch base with current ones, and occasionally volunteer your company's services or products to local fund raising events to build goodwill and prove that you're an active member of the community.

Expect that your need for information and personal contact will shift as your business develops and as you pass through the seasons of your life. A mother of young children may focus on child care and developing relationships with a few clients. Ten years later, that same woman is the mother of teens. Now used to a quiet house (at least during the day), she may want to increase her workload to save for looming college tuition. She may spend much of her time prospecting new clients face-to-face, and the contact may not drain her emotionally as it would have when her children were preschoolers.

If you are apprehensive about a particular aspect of working from home—say, how to rearrange your family's expectations of how you're spending your time, or how to get and stay organized, try to link up with someone who is strong where you are weak.

While mentoring is a well-established way of advancing in the nine to five corporate world, it's rare for home workers to have that kind of relationship. Nevertheless, if you determine that you need a helping hand or someone to whom you are accountable as you are establishing your home-work situation, pray that the Lord will bring that person to you. While you're praying, try to determine if you need mentoring for the work-from-home life-style or for the particular field you are pursuing.

If you struggle with issues of self-discipline, you may be able to get the guidance you need from a well-organized veteran homemaker who has been juggling family, church, and volunteer responsibilities for decades—even if she hasn't been working for pay. Such a person may be willing to hold you accountable for how you spend all of your time, enabling you to manage your days effectively.

On the other hand, if you need help with a particular aspect of running a business—for instance, overseeing your assistant or establishing smooth procedures for taking and filling mail orders—then pursue someone who is functioning well in that area. That individual may or may not be a Christian, and may not even be in your exact line of work. (In fact, I definitely recommend not asking a direct competitor to hold your hand!) What you are looking for is an operational example to follow.

For instance, when the new owners of the travel newsletter told me that they were increasing the number of pages by 50 percent, doubling the number of Midwest states we covered, and giving me a budget to hire free-lancers, all at the same time, I was forced to reconfigure my entire approach to editorial planning. I had to find and manage qualified writers, figure out how to keep track of in-process assignments up to eight issues in advance; and make sure that the stories fit the newsletter's style—effective immediately.

I solved much of this on my own, but the slippery organizational issue of keeping track of all the work-in-process had me stymied. A couple of conversations with an editor whose organizational skills I admire gave me enough insight to invent a system that appears to work—so far. Her encouragement also helped me recognize that much of my intuition about handling my expanded responsibilities was correct. I just needed to hear that encouragement from someone I knew and respected.

The Ultimate Job Description

Your career can be a welcome antidote to the emotional and spiritual complications of being a spouse, parent, Christian, and friend. It's a challenge not to let your life be defined by what you do in most of these arenas; isn't it a relief to be able to do just that with your career?

Go ahead and have fun with the work that the Lord has set before you. Pray that He'll use your job to help you grow in ways that might not be addressed by other avenues. Likewise, expect that the experience you gain in managing time, money, projects, and people will eventually be put to Kingdom purposes! (After all, if you can successfully provide direction and oversight to an ornery group of staffers on a work project, pulling together volunteers for the church nursery should be a piece of cake.)

When I get to heaven, I don't expect that many of my stories or books (okay, maybe this one) will be on the shelves of the celestial library. But I do expect to see the complete fruits of my efforts from God's point of view: character and discipline developed through work projects, blessings brought to my family because of the faith I've demonstrated to Mark and my girls, people whose faith I've built through example and encouragement. I hope you and I alike will be able to look back on the whole of the our lives and know that we were, with all that God gave us, good and faithful servants.

Resources

Please remember that while this information has been double-checked, prices, addresses, and phone numbers do change.

Books

Try to track down a book that addresses the specific knowledge gaps that you've pinpointed. If you still feel unsure about the mechanics of working from home, pick up a how-to-start-a-small-business guide. You're likely to get better advice from such a guide, written by bona fide accountants and lawyers, than from a general book on "starting a home business" from a self-appointed expert.

What you want is a good how-to guide, and the quality of the advice should not be lower just because of the location of your company. As well, be aware that many how-to home business guides will be able to address in only the most general terms zoning, taxes, finances, and other purely local issues. You will still have to do quite a bit of homework to get specific answers to comply with state and local laws and to fit your particular situation.

If you're fairly confident of your business direction, skip the general books and get those that address the start-up issues pertinent to your field or fill gaps in your knowledge or experience: financing, marketing, operations, guides to home-based franchises, mail-order, or other specific topics.

You may get a solid start from these books, or they may simply equip you to ask intelligent questions as you narrow down the options on, say, determining the right configuration of personal computer and peripherals for your needs.

A guide to doing business in your state is essential. (Ignorance of the law is no defense against breaking the law.) Check in bookstores or the book section of an office supply superstore for a notebook-type book on getting started in your particular state, such as *Starting and Operating a Business in Illinois, a Step-by-Step Guide*.

To find the volume for your state, contact Oasis Press, 300 North Valley Drive, Grants Pass, OR 97526 (503)479-9464. The series covers advantages and disadvantages of the basic types of ownership; how to write a business plan; licenses you'll have to get; employee related paperwork; taxes, state laws and regulations for starting home businesses; and basic accounting and small-business tax guidelines.

One last caveat: beware of "opportunity" books and magazines. This is a whole genre of "get rich quick" schemes. That's not to say that the ideas they tout are illegal. It's just that these volumes report in breathless, undiscriminating tones on a myriad of supposedly successful entrepreneurs and offer, at best, only the barest idea of the practical aspects of starting and operating the businesses they profile.

High on my caution list in this category are books that purport to give you hundreds of ideas for home-based businesses. These will range from the mundane (pet sitting) to the unlikely (copy shop—I've never seen one based from home and I suspect it's illegal just about everywhere) with a whole range in between. The worst of these books offer only a paragraph on each idea. If you are truly bereft of inspiration and are hoping that you'll hit on a couple of concepts you can research, at least get a book that provides several resources on each opportunity listed.

250 Home-Based Jobs: Innovative, Imaginative Alternatives to the World of 9 to 5!, Scott Olson, Prentice Hall Press, Simon & Schuster, 1990.

If you're short on ideas, this book could spark some creative juices. Its approach is a bit simplistic, listing everything from short-haul trucking to occupations that require innate skill, like being a caricature artist or a kayak builder, and estimates of start-up costs are too low. The book does include resource lists for each of the occupations listed, but provides very little in the way of product or service pricing or income potential.

900 Know-How, How to Succeed With Your Own 900 Number Business, Robert Mastin, Aegis Publishing Group, Newport RI, 1992.

Hands-on guide to becoming an "infopreneur" by exploiting phone technology to sell niche information.

The Best Home-based Franchises, Gregory Matusky and the Philip Leif Group, Doubleday, 1992

This book provides a thorough explanation of franchising and lots of tips on how to evaluate a franchiser. The franchise listings are well researched.

The Best Home Businesses for the 90s, Paul and Sarah Edwards, Jeremy P. Tarcher, Inc., 1991.

Outstanding list of businesses and self-employment concepts that will help you match your skills with market needs. Included are estimated start-up costs and details of the knowledge and skills you need to have to qualify for each job. The Edwardses also provide estimates of how much you can make at each job and resources for finding out more on each concept are listed.

From Kitchen to Market, Selling Your Gourmet Food Specialty, Stephen Hall, Upstart Publishing Company, Inc., Dover, NH, 1992.

Very detailed advice on analyzing the market for, and taking the first steps in getting a specialty food item from stove to store.

Home Business Big Business, Mel Cook, Collier Books/MacMillan Publishing Co. 1992.

This is a guidebook for the very ambitious. It includes lots of profiles of "million-dollar home businesses" that are now recognizable national operations like Mary Kay, Lillian Vernon and Discovery Toys. The book includes lots of first person advice from CEOs of major corporations who started in their homes. The chapter on pricing and cost analysis is excellent.

How to Run Your Own Home Business, Coralee Smith, Kern & Tammara Hoffman Wolfgram, VGM Career Horizons, 1992.

This basic work-from-home guide includes a number of helpful worksheets for analyzing your strengths, goal making, and elementary financial planning.

Making It On Your Own, Sarah and Paul Edwards, Jeremy P. Tarcher, 1991.

Sarah Edwards, a psychologist, discusses the paycheck mentality, and the process of shifting expectations and work habits to a home-work or entrepreneurial situation. The authors explain motivational techniques and how to deal with emotional issues (fear, anger, disappointment, and so on).

Read this book if you need more tools to get in shape psychologically to tackle working from home. I especially like their checkpoints for "How to Know if You're Doing a Good Job."

Marketing for the Home-Based Business, Jeffrey P. Davidson, Bob Adams, Inc. Publishers, 1990.

Provides some excellent suggestions for initiating marketing and selling ideas—a smattering of specific ideas but not much strategy. The author's comments on exploiting technology for maximum marketing impact are helpful.

The Part-time Solution, Charlene Canape, Harper & Row, 1990.

Excellent book, with extremely detailed advice on how to structure and sell a part-time or work-from-home proposal to your current boss.

Working From Home, by Paul and Sarah Edwards, Jeremy P. Tarcher, 1990.

The Edwardses, probably the most prominent work-from-home advocates on a national scale, consistently turn out excellent primers on working from home. They pay lots of attention to the "human side" and wisely don't get in over their heads advising readers on technological, financial, and tax matters.

Working Moms, From Survival to Satisfaction, Miriam Neff, NavPress, 1992.

A good "perspective" book—Neff examines assumptions in the Christian subculture about working mothers, women's roles, and seasons of life. The book is geared for those working in a traditional corporation or institution.

Periodicals

You'll need to stay current in your field, as well as keep abreast of general business and technological trends. If you are very pressed for time, don't know many other home workers, or live in a remote area, you may want to consider a home-work specialty newsletter.

However, be aware that these are not good sources for up-to-the-minute small business news and trends.

ArtCrafters, a quarterly, lists upcoming arts and craft fairs and includes articles on marketing handmade items. 3200 Irvin Cobb Drive, Paducah, KY 42003 (502) 444-6212 (800) 755-0226.

ConneXions covers the whole spectrum of work-at-home options, from entrepreneurs to telecommuting. Editor Caroline Hull provides practical information, profiles of successful home workers, and loads of networking opportunities. She also organized MATCH, a suburban Washington, D.C.-area support network for professional women who are working from home. P.O. Box 1461, Manassas, VA 22110 (703) 791-6264 FAX (703) 791-2442.

Crafts Report is more sophisticated than *ArtCrafters*, providing in-depth trends and how-to articles on marketing arts and crafts. It's published monthly; a one-year subscription is $24. The Crafts Report Publishing Co., Inc., P.O. Box 1992, 700 Orange St., Wilmington, DE 19801 (302) 656-2209 (800) 777-7098.

Home Office Computing is probably the best all-around home business magazine for anyone whose computer is the heart of their operation. The title is a little misleading, because this is not a magazine for techies. You'll find plenty of articles on marketing, taxes, and trends, all with a home-office focus. The common thread is lots of advice on how to make microcomputer technology work its very hardest for you. For subscription information: P.O. Box 2511, Boulder, CO 80302 (800) 678-0118.

HomeWork Newsletter, published by Gregg Harris (who runs the Christian Life workshops) provides a bimonthly dose of Christian encouragement and homilies for work-from-home entrepreneurs, particularly mothers with children at home and those with crafts, food, or other very locally oriented businesses. It's most valuable for the short profiles of successful businesses, complete resource lists, and good marketing and networking tips. An annual subscription is $20. P.O. Box 2250, Gresham, OR 97030 (503) 667-3942.

Inc. The Magazine for Growing Companies. Inc. has the market on sharp, challenging small-business guidance cornered. Loads of practical advice, in-depth profiles of winners and losers, and focused analysis of business trends. *Inc.* is aimed for top management of fast-growth companies and very ambitious entrepreneurs. While it's almost always a good read, it may be overkill for those who are aiming for a low-key, part-time home career. The magazine offers a unique service: *Inc.* on Demand, an automated order service through which anyone can order past articles for $8.95 each. This is invaluable for researching potential clients, pinpointing industry trends, and getting specific information on management issues. Call (800) 995-4455 to tap into the service. For subscription information: P.O. Box 54129, Boulder CO 80322-4129 (800) 234-0999.

Keyboard Connections offers excellent detailed how-to, marketing, financial analysis articles and entrepreneur profiles, all targeted to home-based desktop graphics and office support businesses. A four-issue annual subscription is $25. Contact Editor Nancy Malvin, *Keyboard Connections*, P.O. Box 338-JNC, Glen Carbon, IL 62034 (618) 667-4666 FAX (618) 667-8002.

National Home Business Report is a quarterly by Barbara Brabec, a self-appointed expert in home business. Her chatty style seems to encourage networking for home workers. The articles provide general, not terribly sophisticated observations and advice on everything from marketing to tax trends. Some advice is misguided at best. It's most valuable for craft entrepreneurs. Barbara Brabec Productions, P.O. Box 2137, Naperville, Ill. 60567

Brabec is also author of *Homemade Money, Creative Cash, Crafts Marketing Success Secrets*, and several other books written at the same level as her newsletter.

Successful Home Business magazine, a quarterly, tends to be filled with get-rich-quick schemes and lots of case histories (one recent issue profiled a snail farmer). If you're searching for ideas, take a look, but don't rely on *Successful Home Business* for ongoing advice.

The Wall Street Journal. Find some way to take a daily look at *The Wall Street Journal,* even if you have to persuade your spouse to bring home the office copy. The $150 or so annual price for daily home delivery is steep, but subscribe as soon as you can afford it. Otherwise, you'll be reacting to trends, not anticipating them.

A careful reading of the *Journal* will keep you abreast of business news and trends, which you should be able to translate to marketing opportunities and other fresh ideas for work.

That's also why you should read the weekly business paper for your area and at least one general business magazine like *Business Week*, *Forbes*, or *Fortune*.

Working Woman is invaluable for anyone whose situation is closely entwined with the traditional corporate environment, like telecommuting, job sharing, and flex time. The articles are timely and useful; beware of the sometimes overbearing feminist point of view. For subscription information, contact the magazine at P.O. Box 3276, Harlan, IA 51593-2456.

Associations

Home by Choice is a national network of Christian mothers who have chosen to stay home with their young children. Many of them work part-time from home, and the association's newsletter, *Table Talk*, (bimonthly, $15 annually) could be used as a limited networking source. P.O. Box 103, Vienna, VA 22183.

Mother's Home Business Network offers several manuals, a newsletter called *Homeworking Mothers*, and networking with other members. Membership is $19. P.O. Box 423, East Meadow, NY 11554 (516) 997-7394.

National Association for the Cottage Industry was founded by Coralee Smith Kern, one of the "founding mothers" of the home-business movement. Membership is $45 annually and includes a subscription to the quarterly magazine *Cottage Connection* as well as other benefits. P.O. Box 14850, Chicago, IL 60614 (312) 472-8116.

National Association for Female Executives gives materials and advice on developing and critiquing business plans. Occasionally the association makes "seed money" loans to start-up ventures. Membership costs $29 and includes a subscription to the bimonthly magazine *Executive Female*. 127 West 24th St., New York, NY 10011 (212) 645-0770.

National Association of Business Owners offers its members extensive opportunities to get involved with political and management issues via task forces and work groups. Local chapter meetings are a great place to network and make contacts with potential clients. Dues are established by the chapters, and range from $60 to about $100 annually. 600 S. Federal St., #400, Chicago, IL 60605 (312) 922-0465.

Women in Business includes entrepreneurs as well as executives in corporate and non-profit circles in southern California. It offers small group and mentoring programs, as well as networking opportunities. 7080 Hollywood Boulevard, Suite 410, Los Angeles, CA 90028 (213) 461-2936.

Catalogs

If you're unable to track down books that provide specific information, try one of these mail-order sources.

The Entrepreneur's Business Success Resource Guide, Aegis Publishing Group, 796 Aquidneck Ave., Newport, RI 02840.

Mother & Home Books offers a rich selection of how-to and inspirational books on very specific work-at-home topics, like running a mail-order business. Many of the books are written by Christians. Proprietor Jessica Leggett is willing to advise on choosing the right books for your needs. Westerdale Rd., RR 2, Box 1228, Woodstock, VT 05091 (802) 457-1993.

The Whole Work Catalog offers a broad spectrum of books and other resources on alternative work styles, including entrepreneurship, working at home, and guides to developing specific careers such as arts management, operating a bed-and-breakfast, or working as a manufacturer's rep. Request a copy from the New Careers Center, Inc., 1515-23rd St., P.O. Box 297, Boulder CO 80306 (303) 447-1087.

Consulting

The Career Action Center offers a variety of career counseling, resources, and career exploration services. It specializes in addressing women's career concerns. 445 Sherman Ave., Palo Alto, CA 94306 (415) 324-1710 FAX (415) 324-9357.

Homemakers Organization for Productive Enterprise is headed by Donata Glassmeyer, a home-based business consultant who operates seminars and workshops and aids home businesses with marketing and publicity plans. She can be reached at 7172 Striker Rd., Maineville, OH, 45039 (513) 583-9839.

Myerson Smagley, Inc. is a human resource consulting and career development firm with experience in helping women negotiate permanent part-time professional work. 923 Marion Ave., Highland Park, IL 60035 (312) 263-6262.

Part Time Resources offers one-on-one consulting for those seeking permanent, career-track part-time work, or for those developing a plan to present to a current employer to switch to part-time, telecommuting, flextime, job sharing or other nontraditional arrangements. The base fee for an hour and a half phone conference is $100. Help writing résumés, cover letters and other material is additional. 399 E. Putnam Ave., Cos Cobs, Conn. 06807 (203) 629-3255.

Governmental Resources

Be sure to check with your municipal zoning authorities about zoning ordinances where you live. Typical restrictions include banning use of a garage or backyard structures as a warehouse; more than twelve customers or clients coming to the house in a twenty-four hour period; and banning more than two non-family employees.

If you are re-entering the job force after an extended absence, contact the national office of the Displaced Homemakers Network. Request information on local seminars, workshops, and networking opportunities. National Displaced Homemakers Network, Suite 300, 1625 K St., NW, Washington, D.C. 20006.

The IRS wants to be your friend. To get a copy of Publication 587, "The Business Use of Your Home," call (800) 829-1040.

The Small Business Administration: you either love it or hate it. If you're a novice considering become self-employed or starting your own company, you may find the SBA's publications, prerecorded information, and consulting service with retired corporate executives (SCORE) helpful. If you've been on your own for a while, or if you're fresh from a corporate environment, you're likely to find the SBA's boot-camp approach a waste of time.

To find out what the SBA has to offer, call 800-827-5722. Inquire about the Small Business Development Center nearest you, where you can pick up publications, take courses, get free advice, and get specific information on women's business ownership.

Other Resources

The Bureau of National Affairs, a private research and publishing group, offers a variety of technical articles and guidelines regarding the ins and outs of independent contractor status. A package of material on the issue can be had for $23 plus $5 shipping and handling. Contact the BNA at 1231 25th St., NW, Washington, D.C. 20037 (800) 452-7773; (202) 452-4323.

Christian Life Workshops are headed by Gregg Harris, a home-schooling and home-business advocate who periodically holds how-to-get-started seminars around the country. He offers a sound Biblical grounding for operating a home business that includes the whole family, as well as insight into Biblical financial planning. You can order the seminar on tape, including notes, for $50. Contact CLW at P.O. Box 2250, Gresham, OR 97030 (503) 677- 3942.

Christian Working Woman is a source of insightful radio broadcasts on cassette tape, that are geared to help Christian women maintain a godly character in the workplace. For more information, contact CWW at P.O. Box 1210, Wheaton, IL 60189 (708) 462-0552.

Coopers and Lybrand, the national accounting firm, offers a $10 Growth Company Starter Kit. It's essentially a primer on how to write a business plan, acquire financing, and begin operating a small business. Most metropolitan areas have a Coopers office; contact the partner in charge of Emerging Business Services to request a copy of the kit.

To order a copy of the DISC test mentioned in chapter 3, contact: **Dr. Michael Roche & Associates,** 115 Simpson St., Geneva, IL 60134 (708) 232-6270. The test costs $7 and an accompanying cassette series, which gives extended commentary on the work preferences revealed by the test, is $30.

Paladin Human Resource Consulting offers advice on sorting out the intricacies of independent contractor situations. For $5, you can buy the company's diagnostic checklist. Address your inquiry to Mr. William Kuzmin, Jr. 22 Bordeaux Drive., Flanders, NJ 07836 (201) 584-9488.

To track down courses, seminars, and other learning opportunities where you can get up to speed in basic accounting, using computers, and other specific business skills, start with your local high school's continuing education department and with your local community college. For-profit learning centers, like the Learning Annex, offer courses generally taught by consultants or moonlighting teachers who may be able to direct you to additional resources or potential employers or clients. Another place to check is the extension service of your state university or college system.

Local chambers of commerce vary widely in their sophistication and depth. Some offer a wide selection of networking opportunities and seminars on small business and operational issues. If your chamber doesn't offer such services, at least pump it for referrals to other business associations that do. Many areas have metropolitan, regional or state business associations that spearhead all sorts of training, educational, networking and lobbying efforts. If your local chamber is clueless, try the membership office of the state chamber. You'll probably find it in your state's capital.

	Primary Wage Earner	Second Wage Earner	Total
Can You Afford Not To Work - Worksheet			
Gross Earnings			
Payroll Taxes *			
Federal Taxes			
FICA			
FICA-Medicare			
State			
Other			
Tithe			
Mortgage/Rent			
Utilities			
Savings - General			
Savings - Retirement			
Auto Expenses/Travel			
Loan Repayment			
Insurance			
Gas			
Maintenance			
Parking/Tolls/Commute			
Insurance			
Auto			
Life			
Homeowners			
Other			
Food			
Medical/Dental			
Clothing			
Dry Cleaning/Laundry			
School /Training			
Gifts/Christmas and Other			
Home Improvement Costs			
Other Loan Repayment			
Entertainment			
Vacation			
Child Care			
Household Help			
Restaurant/Takeout Meals			
Stress Spending			
Miscellaneous			
Total Surplus/Deficit			

*Remember to Increase Tax Amount with second income source.

Business Start-up Costs - To Setup			
Funiture			
Equipment			
Computer			
Software			
Fax			
Telephone			
Files			
Desk(s)			
Shelving/Storage Units			
Assembly/Manufacturing			
Copier			
Telephone Line(s) Installed			
Upgrade of Electrical Service			
Office Build Out			
Business Licenses/Permits			
Legal Fees (Incorporation, Trademark, etc.)			
Accounting Fees			
Business Stationery/Cards			
Logo/graphic creative fee			
Printing			
Mail Box (P.O. Box)			
Yellow Page Listing			
Initial Advertising			
Association Memberships			
Business Equipment Insurance			
Subscriptions - General Business			
- Industry Specific			
Total Start-up Costs			

Business Expense Budget			
	Monthly	Annual	
Salary - Others			
Salary - Owner			
Payroll Taxes			
Fica - Employer			
Workman's Compensation			
Federal Unemployment			
State Unemployment			
Inventory/Cost of Goods			
Accounting Fees			
Advertising			
Auto			
Bank Fees			
Books/Periodicals			
Insurance			
Interest			
Lawyer Fees			
Meals/Entertainment			
Membership/Dues			
Miscellaneous			
Office Supplies			
Postage			
Printing/Reproduction			
Rent			
Taxes			
Telephone			
Training			
Travel			
Utilities			
Total Expenses			
Estimate Sales			
Estimate Gain/(Loss)			